soft furnishing workbooks

lampshades

KatrinCargill

photography by **James Merrell**

RYLAND
PETERS
& SMALL

First Published in Great Britain in 1996

by Ryland Peters & Small

Cavendish House

51-55 Mortimer Street

London W1N 7TD

Text © Katrin Cargill 1996

Design © Ryland Peters & Small 1996

Produced by Mandarin Offset

Printed in Hong Kong

ISBN 1 900518 06 6

A catalogue record for this book is available from the British Library

Art Director **Jacqui Small**

Designer **Ingunn C. Jensen**

Design Assistant **Mark Latter**

Project Editor **Sophie Pearse**

Editorial Assistant **Toria Leitch**

Production **Vincent Smith, Kate MacKillop**

Illustrator **Michael Hill**

DTP Manager **Caroline Wollen**

The publishers have made every effort to ensure that all instructions given in this book regarding potential fire hazard are accurate and safe, but they cannot accept liability for any resulting injury, damage or loss to person or property, whether direct or consequential, and howsoever arising.

contents

once you start looking at people's lamps and what they put
on them you quickly realise that the lampshade is one of the last things to
be considered in a room. Get the walls right, buy the furniture,
mortgage yourself for the curtains, maybe find a good lamp base or two
and that's it, most people have run out of steam. So it's time to give the
poor lampshade a thought or two. Most people's solution is a quick trip to a
department store for a supply of card shades, which are usually the wrong
size for the lamps. I can't walk into a room any more without being drawn
instantly to what's on the lamps, and our own house now has an ever-
changing array of prototypes in different fabrics.

The mood of a room can be instantly changed by the addition of the right
lampshade, the right light and the right amount of it. New technology in
lighting has meant that not only can you control your environment better
with lighting, but dotting around a few well-chosen lamps and shades can
create little areas of cosiness and interest within a room. Colour schemes
can be enhanced with the right shade and a silk taffeta shade for, example,
can add a touch of real luxury. Shapes are an area to look at – mostly we get
the standard coolie or Empire shape, when maybe a tapered box shape
would best suit the base. This book is full of ideas for shapes and sizes,
trimmings and fabrics to inspire you to remedy that all too often neglected
part of home decorating, and there are clear step-by-step instructions for
making your own lampshades. You will also find, as I did, that there are a
surprising number of trained lampshade makers around who can make
some of the ideas shown in the book.

Katrin Cargill

left A three-dimensional pinch-pleated ruffle border sits on the widely flaring rim of a bowed oval shade (seen in full opposite), emphasizing the exaggerated curve.
below Gathered silk covers a basic square frame.

shapes

Lampshades come in all manner of shapes and the outline of the basic frame is what gives the shade its intrinsic character. There are plenty of shapes to choose from – including drums and cylinders; cones of all sorts, from the more open Empire and coolie to the tall narrow chimney; bowed shades with a concave profile; or more solid looking straight-sided shades which may be hexagonal or more box-like, in the form of a gently tapering square or rectangle.

clockwise from top Pale cream and neutral colours in plain silk show off stylish shapes: a waisted square, bordered in a darker contrasting trim; a six-panelled hexagonal star frame; tapering sides and a neat band at the base lift a square frame; neat gathers caught in a collar; an unusual bell shape, completely covered in at the top.

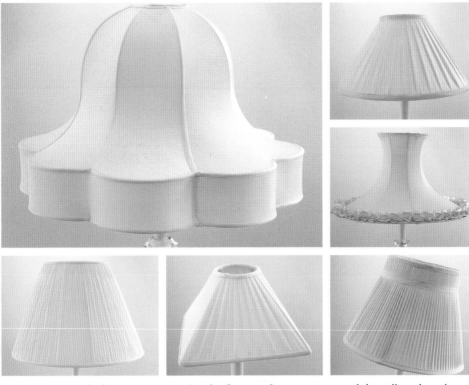

clockwise from top An impressively large covered bell shade with a deeply banded base – a sturdy frame and a very pretty shape for a floor lamp; the standard coolie shape, like this gathered shade, works in any size, for floors or for tables; a wide bowed oval with a narrow waist and a ruffled edge (detail shown opposite); a collared Empire shade, finished with a plain band at the top and bottom and round the collar; pleated cotton flares out from a narrow circular opening at the top to a wider square base; a basic straight-sided Empire shade shows off tightly gathered silk to its best effect.

clockwise from top This elegant wavy edged frame is covered in tightly pleated silk; an octagonal oblong shape with a Regency feel; a wide hexagonal shade allows plenty of light to shine out – ideal for a floor lamp; a wide gathered silk coolie; neat wide box pleats fan out over an elongated oval shade.

—

laminated
checked square

Cheerful red and white linen is laminated to produce a stiff, square-sided shade. If you use a large-checked fabric try to position the pattern so the checks are centred along the folded edges for a look of symmetry; with smaller-scale patterns such as ginghams the positioning is not as important.

materials & equipment

5 cm (2 in) square wire frame

15 cm (6 in) square wire frame, with gimbal

50 cm (20 in) checked linen, 115 cm (45 in) wide

card for template

25 cm (10 in) self-adhesive lampshade backing, 115 cm (45 in) wide

fabric adhesive

metal straight-edge

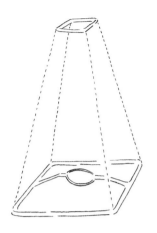

1 Start by making a card template for the shade. Draw one face measuring 25 cm (10 in) in height, 15 cm (6 in) across the bottom and 5 cm (2 in) across the top.

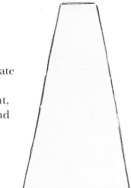

5 Place the laminated fabric right side down on a flat surface. Using the outside edge of the blade of a pair of scissors and a metal straight-edge, score along the pencil lines (made in step 2) marking the four sides of the shade.

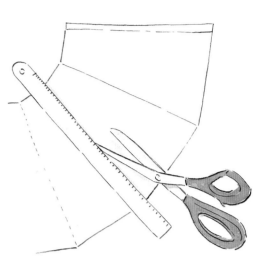

2 Use the template and a pencil to mark the shape of the shade on the self-adhesive backing. Draw one face first and flip the template over to mark the other three with adjoining edges. Draw lines to indicate the folded edges of the shade. Add a 1 cm (½in) seam allowance at one side. Cut one piece.

6 Use the scored lines to create sharp folds at the edges of the shade. To join it up, fold the seam allowance at a 90° angle and run some fabric adhesive down the linen side. Press it to the opposite straight edge, on the inside, and hold until set.

7 To assemble the shade, glue around the bottom inside edge of the shade and the outside edge of the gimbal frame. Insert the frame and hold it in place until set (clothes pegs are handy for holding the frame in position). Repeat for the top frame.

3 Position the backing over the wrong side of the linen with the pattern on the bias. Peel back the laminate and smooth the backing over the fabric.

4 Cut out the laminated fabric, adding an extra ½ cm (¼ in) of linen along the side without a seam allowance. Fold this flap onto the backing and glue it in position.

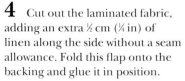

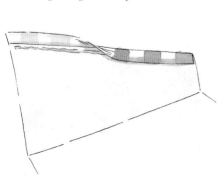

8 To trim the shade and hide the raw edges, make up 84 cm (34 in) of 1 cm (½in) wide bias binding from the linen fabric (see Techniques, page 103). Cut it into two strips for the top and bottom, one measuring 22 cm (9 in) and the other, 62 cm (25 in). Run fabric adhesive along the inside of the binding strips and attach to the top and bottom of the shade, beginning at the join and folding them over the edges as you go. Where the ends meet turn under one of the raw edges and stick it down so that it neatly over-laps the other raw edge. Set the shade on a small base and use a 40-watt golfball bulb.

pleated coolie

A buttery yellow silk taffeta is tightly pleated all round the top of this small coolie, and the pleats fanned out evenly around the gently flaring sides for a crisp clean effect. The lamp is then given a punchy finish with scarlet trimming around the top and bottom rings in the same rich fabric as the main body of the shade, for a strong contrast. The inner silk lining protects the outer cover and gives the whole design a highly professional finish.

materials & equipment

coolie frame with six struts and base gimbal fitting: 10 cm (4 in) diameter top; 25 cm (10 in) diameter bottom; 13 cm (5 in) height

50 cm (20 in) silk lining, 115 cm (45 in) wide

25 cm (10 in) butter-yellow silk taffeta, 150 cm (60 in) wide

92 x 8 cm (36 x 3 in) strip of red silk taffeta

1 cm (½ in) wide binding tape

basic sewing kit (see page 98)

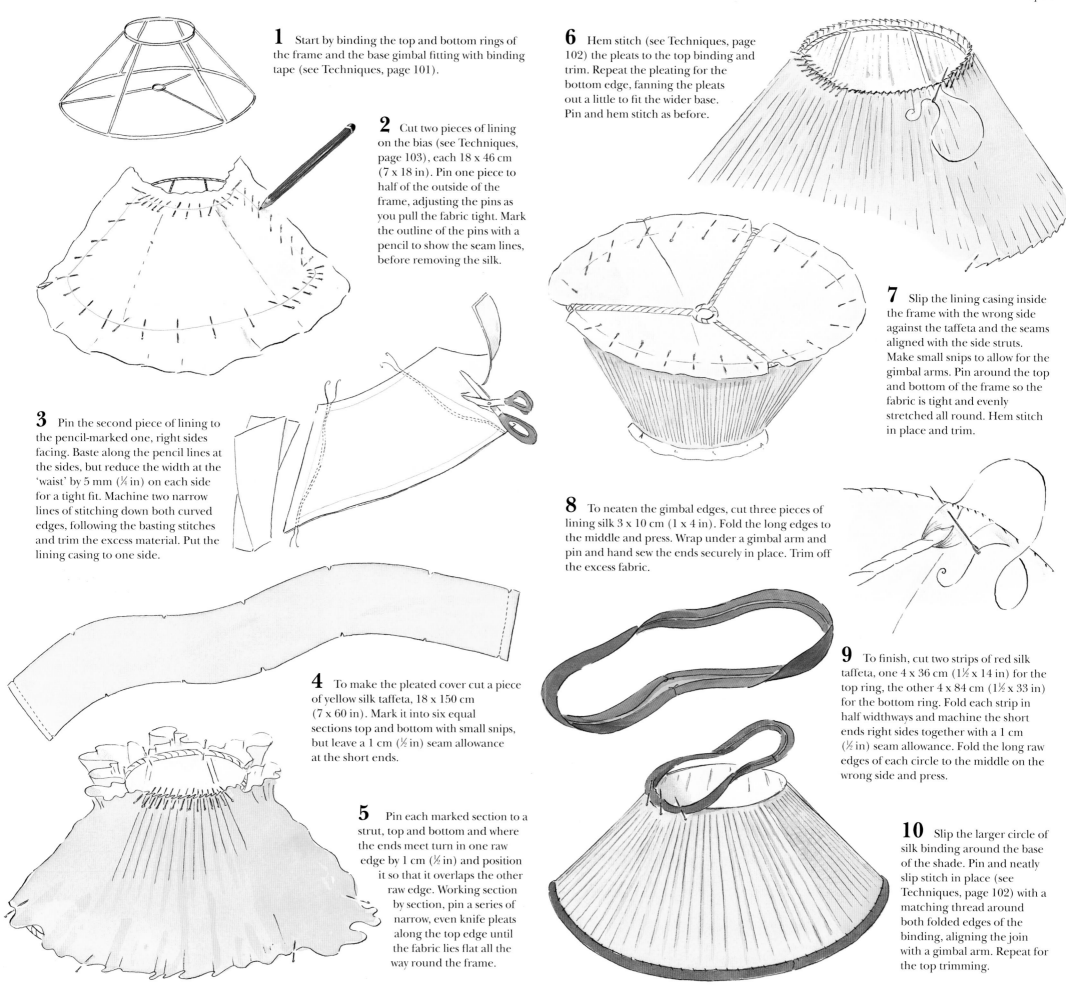

1 Start by binding the top and bottom rings of the frame and the base gimbal fitting with binding tape (see Techniques, page 101).

2 Cut two pieces of lining on the bias (see Techniques, page 103), each 18 x 46 cm (7 x 18 in). Pin one piece to half of the outside of the frame, adjusting the pins as you pull the fabric tight. Mark the outline of the pins with a pencil to show the seam lines, before removing the silk.

3 Pin the second piece of lining to the pencil-marked one, right sides facing. Baste along the pencil lines at the sides, but reduce the width at the 'waist' by 5 mm (¼ in) on each side for a tight fit. Machine two narrow lines of stitching down both curved edges, following the basting stitches and trim the excess material. Put the lining casing to one side.

4 To make the pleated cover cut a piece of yellow silk taffeta, 18 x 150 cm (7 x 60 in). Mark it into six equal sections top and bottom with small snips, but leave a 1 cm (½ in) seam allowance at the short ends.

5 Pin each marked section to a strut, top and bottom and where the ends meet turn in one raw edge by 1 cm (½ in) and position it so that it overlaps the other raw edge. Working section by section, pin a series of narrow, even knife pleats along the top edge until the fabric lies flat all the way round the frame.

6 Hem stitch (see Techniques, page 102) the pleats to the top binding and trim. Repeat the pleating for the bottom edge, fanning the pleats out a little to fit the wider base. Pin and hem stitch as before.

7 Slip the lining casing inside the frame with the wrong side against the taffeta and the seams aligned with the side struts. Make small snips to allow for the gimbal arms. Pin around the top and bottom of the frame so the fabric is tight and evenly stretched all round. Hem stitch in place and trim.

8 To neaten the gimbal edges, cut three pieces of lining silk 3 x 10 cm (1 x 4 in). Fold the long edges to the middle and press. Wrap under a gimbal arm and pin and hand sew the ends securely in place. Trim off the excess fabric.

9 To finish, cut two strips of red silk taffeta, one 4 x 36 cm (1½ x 14 in) for the top ring, the other 4 x 84 cm (1½ x 33 in) for the bottom ring. Fold each strip in half widthways and machine the short ends right sides together with a 1 cm (½ in) seam allowance. Fold the long raw edges of each circle to the middle on the wrong side and press.

10 Slip the larger circle of silk binding around the base of the shade. Pin and neatly slip stitch in place (see Techniques, page 102) with a matching thread around both folded edges of the binding, aligning the join with a gimbal arm. Repeat for the top trimming.

16

tall madras bowed oval

The irregular checks of a fresh green madras cotton sit well on the concave surface of this elegant bowed shade. The slender 'waist' is emphasized by the strips of bias binding down the sides which also neatly cover the stitching underneath. To avoid scorching the narrow sides of the shade use a small low-watt chandelier bulb.

materials & equipment

bowed oval frame with six struts and four-armed gimbal: 35 x 21 cm (14 x 8½ in) diameter bottom oval; 20 x 11 cm (8 x 4½ in) diameter top oval; 36 cm (14½ in) height with a narrow 15 cm (6 in) 'waist'

100 cm (40 in) pale green madras cotton, 115 cm (45 in) wide

50 cm (20 in) white silk lampshade lining fabric, 115 cm (45 in) wide

175 cm (70 in) pale green bobble fringe

1 cm (½ in) wide binding tape

tracing paper and pencil

fabric adhesive

basic sewing kit (see page 98)

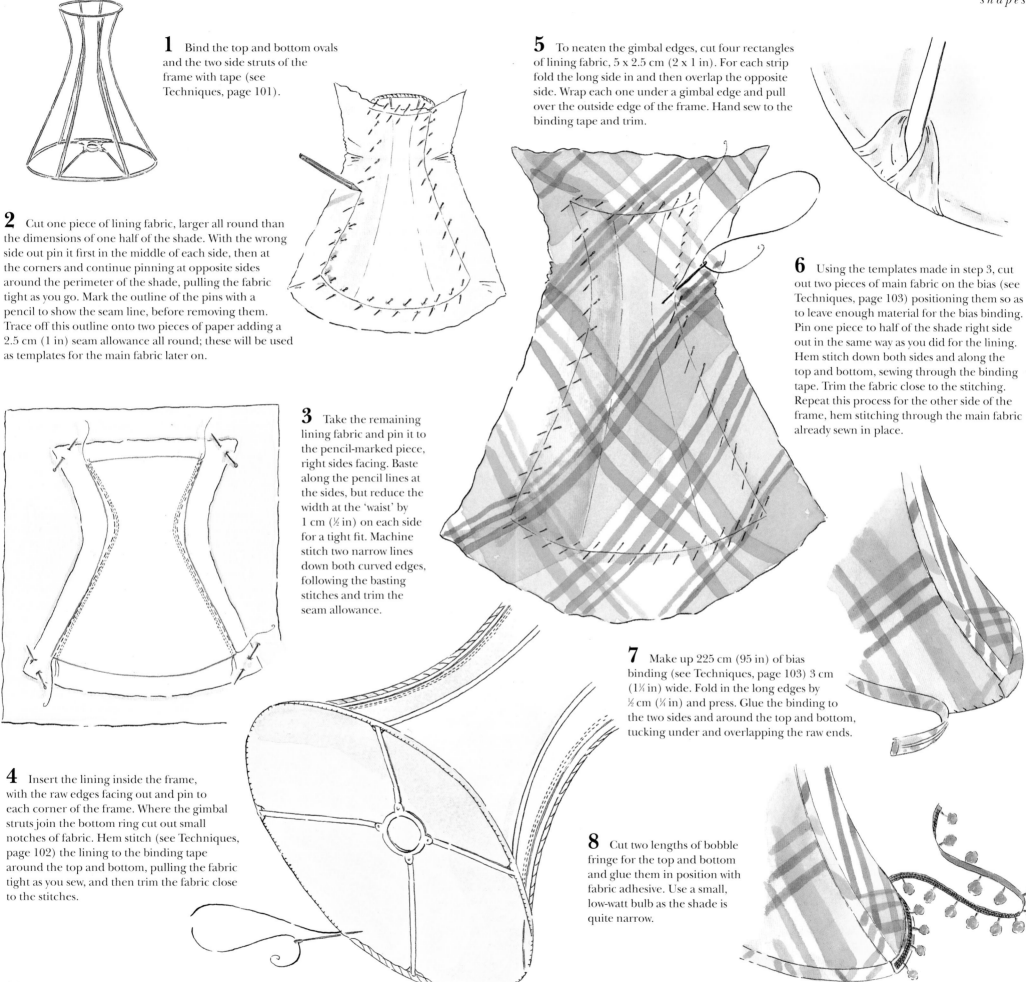

1 Bind the top and bottom ovals and the two side struts of the frame with tape (see Techniques, page 101).

2 Cut one piece of lining fabric, larger all round than the dimensions of one half of the shade. With the wrong side out pin it first in the middle of each side, then at the corners and continue pinning at opposite sides around the perimeter of the shade, pulling the fabric tight as you go. Mark the outline of the pins with a pencil to show the seam line, before removing them. Trace off this outline onto two pieces of paper adding a 2.5 cm (1 in) seam allowance all round; these will be used as templates for the main fabric later on.

3 Take the remaining lining fabric and pin it to the pencil-marked piece, right sides facing. Baste along the pencil lines at the sides, but reduce the width at the 'waist' by 1 cm (½ in) on each side for a tight fit. Machine stitch two narrow lines down both curved edges, following the basting stitches and trim the seam allowance.

4 Insert the lining inside the frame, with the raw edges facing out and pin to each corner of the frame. Where the gimbal struts join the bottom ring cut out small notches of fabric. Hem stitch (see Techniques, page 102) the lining to the binding tape around the top and bottom, pulling the fabric tight as you sew, and then trim the fabric close to the stitches.

5 To neaten the gimbal edges, cut four rectangles of lining fabric, 5 x 2.5 cm (2 x 1 in). For each strip fold the long side in and then overlap the opposite side. Wrap each one under a gimbal edge and pull over the outside edge of the frame. Hand sew to the binding tape and trim.

6 Using the templates made in step 3, cut out two pieces of main fabric on the bias (see Techniques, page 103) positioning them so as to leave enough material for the bias binding. Pin one piece to half of the shade right side out in the same way as you did for the lining. Hem stitch down both sides and along the top and bottom, sewing through the binding tape. Trim the fabric close to the stitching. Repeat this process for the other side of the frame, hem stitching through the main fabric already sewn in place.

7 Make up 225 cm (95 in) of bias binding (see Techniques, page 103) 3 cm (1¼ in) wide. Fold in the long edges by ½ cm (⅛ in) and press. Glue the binding to the two sides and around the top and bottom, tucking under and overlapping the raw ends.

8 Cut two lengths of bobble fringe for the top and bottom and glue them in position with fabric adhesive. Use a small, low-watt bulb as the shade is quite narrow.

above The small coolie-shaped top is edged in a deep band, covered by neat knife pleats of cream silk and lengthened by a silk fringe
right from top Cotton ticking stripes meet perfectly across the angle of this panelled shade to form a chevron design; a lightweight cotton is dipped in fabric stiffener and then diagonally draped over an Empire shade for a ruched effect; rich red crushed velvet is stiffened with lamination and trimmed in leather thonging; the finest ecru silk is tightly gathered around a coolie shade and finished with a pinked skirt; moiré silk in contrasting colours is an ideal choice to complement the shaped panels of this stylish shade.

use of fabrics and trimmings

Second only to the shape of the lampshade, the type of fabric and trimming you choose to cover the frame will dictate the overall look of the shade. For instance, the same basic cone would look very different covered in a laminated striped cloth than if you decided on a loose, skirt-like cover in a floral print. Heavy- and light-weight fabrics alike can be used to decorate lampshades.

left A crisp red-and-white cotton gingham is shown to best effect on a simple Empire shape. The geometric check accentuates the perfect knife pleats, which are finished in a binding of the same checked fabric, used on the diagonal.

below from left Double pinked ruffles in a complementary fabric with a smaller motif edge this tightly gathered, printed cotton shade; delicate cream lace is generously gathered and held in place over a plain cream shade by a pretty satin ribbon tied in a bow; this unusual shade is created using a thin printed cotton which is stiffened with lamination and then scored into shaped sections – bias binding finishes the raw edges and a ribbon threaded through the scored sections pulls the shade into tight gathers to form a petal pattern along the top edge.

above A coolie-shaped frame is covered in a tightly gathered printed cotton, and trimmed along the bottom edge in a strongly contrasting deep cotton fringe.

right Delicate checked voile floats out from a smocked top, used as a loose cover over a collared Empire silk shade. The top and bottom edges are finished in thin red velvet piping.

skirted
pictorial print

Patterned fabrics work as well as plains, particularly on loose fabric lampshades. Here a pretty red and white *toile de Jouy* is sewn into a full, pleated skirt set off with a bold matching trim that sits on the bottom edge. The shade is given added fullness with the addition of an underskirt between the outer cover and the lining.

materials & equipment

frame with six struts and reverse gimbal fitting: 17 cm (7 in) diameter top; 30 cm (12 in) diameter bottom; 20 cm (8 in) height

125 cm (50 in) lining fabric, 115 cm (45 in) wide

100 cm (40 in) toile de Jouy fabric, 140 cm (55 in) wide

140 cm (55 in) coordinating trimming, 3 cm (1½ in) wide

1 cm (½ in) wide binding tape

basic sewing kit (see page 98)

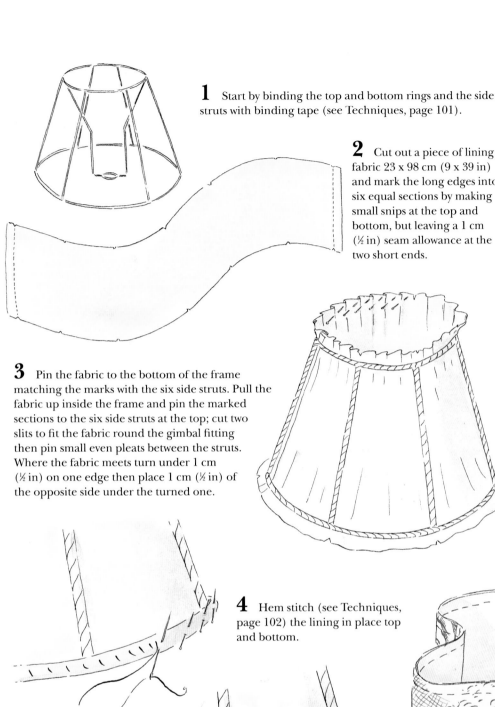

1 Start by binding the top and bottom rings and the side struts with binding tape (see Techniques, page 101).

2 Cut out a piece of lining fabric 23 x 98 cm (9 x 39 in) and mark the long edges into six equal sections by making small snips at the top and bottom, but leaving a 1 cm (½ in) seam allowance at the two short ends.

3 Pin the fabric to the bottom of the frame matching the marks with the six side struts. Pull the fabric up inside the frame and pin the marked sections to the six side struts at the top; cut two slits to fit the fabric round the gimbal fitting then pin small even pleats between the struts. Where the fabric meets turn under 1 cm (½ in) on one edge then place 1 cm (½ in) of the opposite side under the turned one.

4 Hem stitch (see Techniques, page 102) the lining in place top and bottom.

5 Cut a strip of lining on the bias 98 x 2.5 cm (39 x 1 in). Trim the short ends along the straight grain and machine stitch them together, right sides facing and using a seam allowance of 1 cm (½ in); trim the corners. Fold in one edge of the circle by 0.5 cm (¼in) and press, then pin and hem stitch the remaining raw edge around the bottom of the frame. Pull up the folded edge to hide the stitches.

6 Cut out two strips of lining fabric 8 x 4 cm (3 x 1½ in). Fold both long edges to the middle and wrap under each gimbal arm. Pin and neatly hand sew the ends to the top of the frame and trim the excess fabric.

7 Now take a piece of *toile de Jouy* fabric 28 x 200 cm (11 x 80 in); machine stitch panels and the short ends using a 2.5 cm (1 in) seam allowance. Turn under the raw edges on the seam allowance by 0.5 cm (¼ in), press and machine down (do *not* stitch through to the main panel).

8 Turn the bottom edge of the *toile de Jouy* to the right side by 0.5 cm (¼ in) and press. Pin, baste and machine stitch the decorative trim to the right side on the bottom edge, taking in the hem, and hiding all raw edges. Neatly tuck under the ends where they meet.

9 To line the skirt, use a piece of lining fabric 28 x 200 cm (11 x 80 in); join panels where necessary and the short ends using a French seam (see Techniques, page 103) with a total allowance of 2.5 cm (1 in) and press to one side. Turn the bottom edge of the circle to the wrong side making a double 0.5 cm (¼ in) hem; pin and machine stitch in place.

10 Place the right side of the lining casing against the wrong side of the *toile de Jouy*. Pin and baste the raw edges of both layers together 1 cm (½ in) from the top. Pin and baste a series of pleats about 2.5 cm (1 in) wide around the top edge. Slip the skirt over the lined shade and pin to the top of the frame; make any necessary adjustments to the pleats to fit the circumference exactly. Hem stitch in place and trim.

11 Cut a strip of *toile de Jouy* on the bias 60 x 4 cm (24 x 1½ in) and machine stitch the short ends together as in step 5. Turn in one edge by 1 cm (½ in) and press. Pin the remaining raw edge to the frame, right side down and with the binding on the inside; hem stitch in place. Pull the folded edge over the frame to the outside and secure all the way round with a slip stitch (see Techniques, page 102).

hessian
half shade

Here a curvaceous, half floral shade is covered with a coarse hessian. The gimp trim and coiled rope with tassels provide complementary rough textures. Use a low, 25-watt bulb as the hessian has a very loose weave; if you use a higher wattage bulb the shade should be lined.

materials & equipment

half floral frame with five struts and bulb clip: 30 cm(12 in) height; 29 cm (11½ in) width across top; 43 cm (17 in) width across bottom; 8 cm (7 in) width at 'waist'

50 cm (20 in) calico, 115 cm (45 in) wide

50 cm (20 in) hessian, 115 cm (45 in) wide

150 cm (60 in) gimp or hessian braid

50 cm (20 in) rope with tasselled ends

1 cm (½ in) wide binding tape

fabric adhesive

basic sewing kit (see page 98)

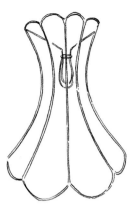

1 First bind the frame along the two outside struts, the central strut and the top and bottom curves (see Techniques, page 101).

2 Cut the calico in half and use one half to make a pattern. Pin the calico to the binding tape on one half of the frame. Start pinning in the middle at the top and bottom, then pin at opposite corners, then work around the sides inserting pins as you go. Use a pencil to mark the outline made by the pins.

3 Remove the pins and marked calico from the frame. Cut out the fabric adding an extra 1 cm (½ in) seam allowance around all outside edges to make a pattern and then make a second one from the other half of the calico. The second pattern should be a mirror image of the first.

4 Position both patterns onto a square of hessian and pin in place. Make sure the patterns lie diagonally across the grain (this will give the hessian better stretch). Cut out two pieces of hessian and discard the patterns.

5 Seam the two hessian pieces together down the centre using a 1 cm (½ in) seam allowance. Make a double row of stitches (or strengthen with overlocking) to prevent fraying (see Techniques, page 103).

6 Carefully position and pin the central seam along the central strut of the frame and continue to pin all round the perimeter of the frame. Insert pins opposite each other all round the frame, pulling the hessian tight as you go.

7 Once the hessian is neatly pinned in place hem stitch (see Techniques, page 102) around the perimeter of the frame to secure. Trim off any excess fabric and frayed edges.

8 Glue the length of gimp or hessian braid around the perimeter of the shade as a trimming and to hide the hem stitches. Fold under the raw end for a neat finish.

9 Finally, coil the rope trim so that both tassels hang evenly and glue the coil firmly to the central strut at the 'waist' of the shade. If necessary secure with a few hand stitches. Choose a bulb with a low wattage to avoid glare, or add an interlining if you prefer.

raw and ruffled

A raw cream silk is perhaps one of the most traditional and widely used lampshade coverings, providing a strong outer casing suitable for direct or indirect lighting and at the same time the rich texture of the fabric adds a sophisticated touch to any room setting. However, here the shade is given an original decorative treatment – the main body of the cone is made up in laminated silk while the top and bottom are trimmed with a double row of raw silk ruffles.

materials & equipment

10 cm (4 in) diameter top ring with reversible gimbal

28 cm (11 in) diameter bottom ring

150 cm (60 in) cream raw silk, 115 cm (45 in) wide

1 cm (½ in) wide binding tape

75 cm (30 in) self-adhesive lampshade backing, 115 cm (45 in) wide

fabric adhesive

paper, ruler, pencil and tape measure

pinking shears

clothes pegs

basic sewing kit (see page 98)

1 Start by binding the top and bottom rings (see Techniques, page 101).

2 For a cone-shaped shade it is necessary to make a pattern. Take a large sheet of thin card and starting in the bottom right-hand corner mark a horizontal line A, equal to the 28 cm (11 in) diameter of the bottom ring. Draw a vertical line B, upwards through the middle of the horizontal one and mark a point 15 cm (6 in), or the height of the shade, above the first one. Centre a second horizontal line C, through this point as long as the diameter of the top ring which in this case is 10 cm (4 in). Draw the sides of the shade, continuing the lines upwards until they meet.

To create the outline of the pattern, pin a length of tape or string to the tip of the triangle and using a pencil attached to the end of the tape draw two arcs; start one at the top right-hand corner of the shade shape and the other at the bottom right-hand corner. The top and bottom arcs should be as long as the circumference of the top and bottom of the shade plus 1 cm (½ in) overlap.

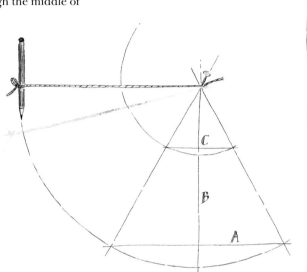

3 Cut out the card template and place it over the lampshade backing. Mark the outline of the template with a pencil and cut one piece.

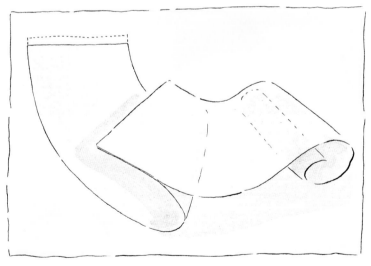

4 Position the backing over the wrong side of the fabric on the bias, making sure you have 50 cm (20 in) of fabric left. Peel back 2.5 cm (1 in) of the backing paper and stick the laminate firmly in place. Carefully pull back the backing paper from under the laminate, making sure the laminate adheres to the fabric smoothly with no creases. You may find it easier to pin the fabric securely in place before you start.

5 Cut out the silk fabric around the backing adding an extra 1 cm (½ in) seam allowance at one of the sides. Dribble a line of fabric adhesive along the wrong side of this seam allowance and stick it to the backing.

6 Before sealing up the side seam, check the fit of the shade around the rings by pegging it in position. Mark the exact position of the overlap and remove the pegs. Now glue the silk overlap to the opposite inside edge of the shade, lining up the marks made, and hold in place until the glue has set.

7 To assemble the shade run a line of glue around the top and bottom inside edges of the cone and around the outside edges of both rings. Insert each ring, lining up the strips of glue and place pegs around the edges to hold the rings in position until the adhesive dries.

8 To trim the bottom edge of the shade cut six strips of silk 86 cm (34 in) long and 5 cm (2 in) wide. Join them together to make two strips, each three times the length of the circumference of the bottom edge. Neaten all the edges with pinking shears and lay the strips on top of one another, right sides up. Sew a line of running stitches along the middle of the strips and pull the stitches into even gathers until the strip fits the bottom ring, leaving a slight overlap. Machine stitch close to the running stitches to secure the gathers. Repeat this process for the top using six strips measuring 30 cm (12 in) long and 4 cm (1 ½ in) wide joined to make two strips three times the circumference.

9 Glue the centre line of the longer frill 1 cm (½ in) above the bottom of the frame, overlapping the ends. Glue the shorter frill 0.5cm (¼in) below the top ring.

10 At intervals of 2 cm (1 in) pinch together the outside edges of the inside frill, top and bottom; secure with a spot of glue.

woven ribbons

Instead of using a panel of fabric, this novel shade is covered with a close basketweave of gingham ribbon. Here only one pattern of ribbon is used but you can choose any sort of ribbon or combination of colours to create your woven shade. Adjust your measurements according to the width of the ribbons used and the size of the frame and follow the simple weaving principle, finishing the top and bottom with a bright contrast trim.

materials & equipment

rectangular frame with curved long sides and reversible top gimbal: 27 x 13 cm (10½ x 5 in) bottom; 16 x 8 cm (6½ x 3 in) top; with 25 cm (10 in) long curved sides and 4 in (10 cm) measurement across the middle, top and bottom

13.5 m (45 ft) gingham ribbon, 2½ cm (1 in) wide

135 cm (4½ ft) contrasting bias binding, 1 cm (½ in) wide

1 cm (½ in) wide binding tape

fabric adhesive

basic sewing kit (see page 98)

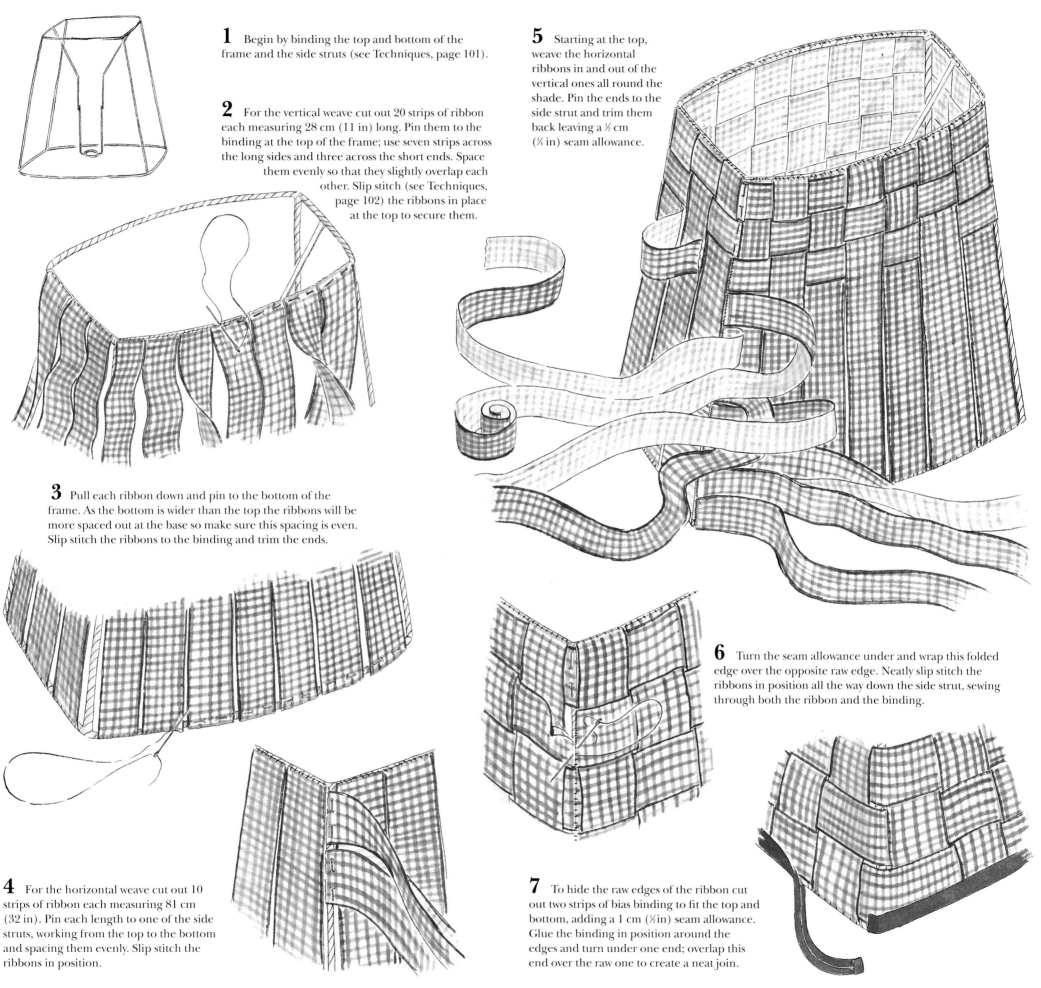

1 Begin by binding the top and bottom of the frame and the side struts (see Techniques, page 101).

2 For the vertical weave cut out 20 strips of ribbon each measuring 28 cm (11 in) long. Pin them to the binding at the top of the frame; use seven strips across the long sides and three across the short ends. Space them evenly so that they slightly overlap each other. Slip stitch (see Techniques, page 102) the ribbons in place at the top to secure them.

3 Pull each ribbon down and pin to the bottom of the frame. As the bottom is wider than the top the ribbons will be more spaced out at the base so make sure this spacing is even. Slip stitch the ribbons to the binding and trim the ends.

4 For the horizontal weave cut out 10 strips of ribbon each measuring 81 cm (32 in). Pin each length to one of the side struts, working from the top to the bottom and spacing them evenly. Slip stitch the ribbons in position.

5 Starting at the top, weave the horizontal ribbons in and out of the vertical ones all round the shade. Pin the ends to the side strut and trim them back leaving a ½ cm (¼ in) seam allowance.

6 Turn the seam allowance under and wrap this folded edge over the opposite raw edge. Neatly slip stitch the ribbons in position all the way down the side strut, sewing through both the ribbon and the binding.

7 To hide the raw edges of the ribbon cut out two strips of bias binding to fit the top and bottom, adding a 1 cm (½ in) seam allowance. Glue the binding in position around the edges and turn under one end; overlap this end over the raw one to create a neat join.

tutu in voile

By loosely gathering the slightly stiff organza material the shade takes on the appearance of a ballerina's tutu and the voile ribbon circling the top gives the whole design delicacy and movement. This pretty shade is surprisingly simple to make, consisting of a plain white lined frame sheathed in a translucent voile; muslin, lace and other sheer fabrics would work just as well, and a different coloured lining could be used to diffuse the light.

materials & equipment

cone-shaped frame with clip fitting and six side struts:
10 cm (4 in) diameter top; 28 cm (11 in) diameter bottom; 17 cm (7 in) height

50 cm (20 in) silk lining fabric, 115 cm (45 in) wide

50 cm (20 in) organza, 150 cm (60 in) wide

1 cm (½ in) wide binding tape

125 cm (50 in) organza ribbon, 4 cm (1½ in) wide

fabric pencil

basic sewing kit (see page 98)

1 Start by binding the rings and the side struts (see Techniques, page 101).

2 Measure and cut a piece of lining fabric 38 x 89 cm (15 x 35½ in). Use your fabric pencil to mark six sections along the length, top and bottom; the sections must be equal in length apart from an additional 1 cm (½ in) seam allowance at the ends. Next mark a line along the centre of the length.

3 Line up this centre line with the bottom ring of the frame and pin it to the binding, turning under and overlapping the side edges where they meet. Slip stitch (see Techniques, page 102) the fabric to the bottom edge, taking the needle through both the fabric and the binding.

4 Taking the silk from the inside first, pull it up and over the top of the frame; match up and pin the six marked sections to the six side struts, making slits to fit the lining around the arms of the clip fitting. Draw the fabric together into small pleats between the struts and pin to the top frame. Hem stitch (see Techniques, page 102) to the top binding; trim.

5 Repeat this process for the silk outer covering but turn under the raw edge around the top for a neat finish.

6 For the decorative cover, cut one piece of organza 32 x 145 cm (13 x 58 in). With right sides together line up the two shorter sides and machine stitch them together using a French seam (see Techniques, page 103).

7 Turn under 1 cm (½ in) twice along one of the longer sides and machine stitch this hem in place.

8 To make the frill, fold 5 cm (2 in) of the unfinished edge to the inside and sew two narrow lines of running stitches close to this edge to form the gathers around the top (see Techniques, page 102).

9 Place the cover over the shade and pull the gathers until they fit the top circumference. Slip stitch it to the lining along the gathered seam.

10 Complete the cover using the length of organza ribbon. Cut the ends diagonally and tie it over the line of gathers on the upper edge of the shade. Now fold the top third of the ribbon over and sew this folded edge to the shade using neat running stitches and following the seam lines on the frill. Tie the loose ends into a bow.

table lamps

This category of lamp covers an overwhelming range to choose from. Styles include slender candlesticks topped with tiny shades; half shades ideal for setting at either end of a mantel piece or on narrow shelving; heavy urn-like bases carrying sizeable shades that may sit on a coffee or side table to provide pools of soft, atmospheric light; reading lights set upon a desk; or pretty dressing-table or bedside lights suitable for the bedroom.

left A white plaster base with a cone shade, laminated with a bright blue polka dot weave. *below from left* White spotted muslin, finished with a ruffle; a generous Provençal cotton-skirt, gathered with a bow; floral cotton, laminated onto a coolie shape, over a classical glass column base.

above A tall turned base, topped with a gathered shade in thin blue woven cotton. *right* A versatile brass table lamp, with maximum manoeuvrability, with a beautifully finished box-pleated shade.

44

above Pretty and practical: a tilt-top desk lamp with a collared shade is finished in a gathered double ruffle.

left, top to bottom A gathered coolie with a difference – pale yellow silk is knife pleated and finished in a blue binding, which is picked up by the matching two-toned deep fringe; striped fabric, neatly box pleated over an Empire shade, is finished in a strong complementary bias binding; a narrow tapered oblong is a good shape to use when there is not much space available, such as on a mantelpiece.

above Polka dotted voile, tightly gathered over this Empire shade, lets out maximum light; the top and bottom edges of this shade have been smartly finished with pinch-pleated silk and a contrasting colour threaded through it.

below A traditional bouillotte tole lamp looks fresh with a pair of blue-and-white striped gathered shades.

box-pleated conical shade

Hiding an ordinary conical shade is a box-pleated cover made in warm red and yellow *toile de Jouy*. The skirt falls in quite loose folds, allowing the pattern of the fabric to remain visible. The bow is a pretty feature highlighting the waist of the shade, and the ruffled effect of the box pleats at the top.

materials & equipment

frame with six struts and reverse gimbal fitting: 13 cm (5 in) diameter top; 5 cm (10 in) diameter bottom; 17 cm (7 in) height

50 cm (20 in) lining fabric, 115 cm (45 in) wide

150 cm (60 in) toile de Jouy fabric, 115 cm (45 in) wide

1 cm (¹/₂ in) wide binding tape

basic sewing kit (see page 98)

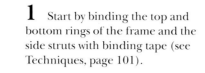

1 Start by binding the top and bottom rings of the frame and the side struts with binding tape (see Techniques, page 101).

2 Cut two pieces of lining, 81 x 20 cm (32½ x 8 in). Mark six equal sections on the long edges top and bottom with small snips but leave an extra 1 cm (½ in) seam allowance at the short ends.

3 Pin one piece of lining fabric to the outside of the frame along the bottom, lining up the marks with the struts. Where the fabric meets fold back the seam allowance on one end and place it so that it overlaps the raw edge on the other side. Pull the fabric up over the frame and start by pinning the marks to the struts, then pin small even pleats between the marks. Hem stitch (see Techniques, page 102) the lining in place and trim.

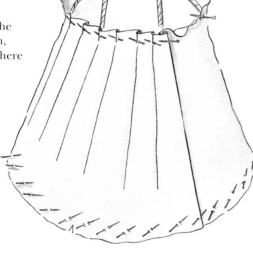

4 Now pin the second piece of lining fabric to the inside of the frame making two small slits at the top to accommodate the gimbal arms. Line up and pin the fabric as in step 3, but at the top and bottom fold under the edge by 0.5 cm (¼ in) positioning it over the existing raw edge for a neat finish. Hem stitch top and bottom and trim.

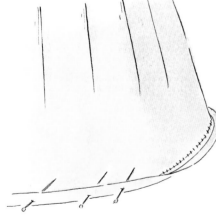

5 To neaten the gimbal arms, cut out two strips of lining fabric 4 x 7 cm (1½ x 2¾ in). Fold both the long edges to the middle and wrap each strip under the gimbal arm. Tuck under the raw edge and pin and hand sew to the top of the frame.

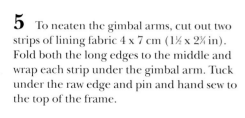

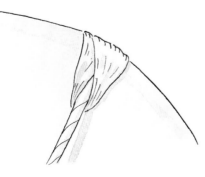

6 For the loose shade, cut out a panel of *toile de Jouy*, 150 x 32 cm (60 x 12½ in), joining pieces and pattern matching as necessary. Fold the panel in half widthways, right sides facing and machine the short ends with a 1.5 cm (⅝ in) seam allowance. To finish the seam turn each side under by 0.5 cm (¼ in) and machine stitch down, making sure you do not sew through to the main fabric.

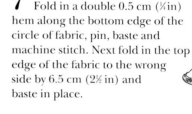

7 Fold in a double 0.5 cm (⅛in) hem along the bottom edge of the circle of fabric, pin, baste and machine stitch. Next fold in the top edge of the fabric to the wrong side by 6.5 cm (2½ in) and baste in place.

8 Make a series of box pleats around the top by folding the material into itself; there should be 12 pleats each with two 2 cm (¾ in) sides and a 4 cm (1½ in) front panel. Pin the pleats and check the fit on the shade, making small adjustments where necessary. Baste and machine stitch the pleats in place 5 cm (2 in) below the top edge.

9 Slip the cover over the frame and sew a line of running stitches (see Techniques, page 102) through all layers, just under the top ring and following the stitches made in step 8.

10 To make the bow, cut out a strip of *toile de Jouy*, 140 x 6.5 cm (55 x 2½ in). If necessary join strips together matching the pattern. Fold in half lengthways with right sides facing and cut the short ends at a slight angle. Machine along the long edge and one of the shorter ones with a 0.5 cm (¼ in) seam allowance.

11 Use a knitting needle or a safely pin to push the fabric right side out through the open end. Tuck the raw ends to the inside and neatly sew the opening closed. Tie into a bow around the top of the frame.

smocked patterned shade

A pretty blue Provençal skirt with a smocked top is slipped over a plain lined shade; the elasticated top ensures that the cover stays firmly in place. Choose any motif pattern as an alternative. The great thing about this practical design is that it can be removed easily to shake the dust off or for washing.

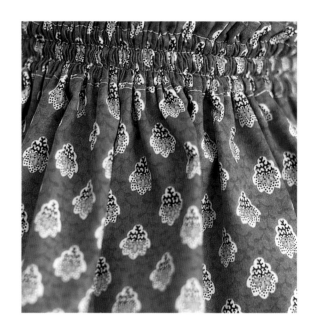

materials & equipment

frame with eight side struts and duplex fitting: 16 cm (6½ in) diameter top; 25 cm (10 in) diameter bottom; 17 cm (7 in) height, including 4 cm (1½ in) collar

125 cm (50 in) lining fabric, 115 cm (45 in) wide

50 cm (20 in) Provençal cotton, 150 cm (60 in) wide

1 cm (½ in) wide binding tape

150 cm (60 in) elastic, 0.5 cm (¼ in) wide

basic sewing kit (see page 98)

1 Start by binding all parts of the frame with binding tape (see Techniques, page 101).

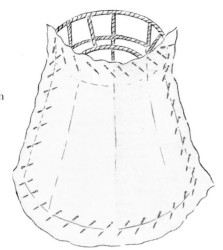

2 Cut four pieces of lining fabric, 20 x 43 cm (8 x 17 in). Pin one to half of the outside of the frame starting in the middle of the top and bottom rings, then at the sides and corners and continue pinning at opposite sides, keeping the fabric tight. Mark the outline of the pins with a pencil before removing the lining from the frame. Using this as a template cut three more pieces of lining fabric, adding a 2.5 cm (1 in) seam allowance around the pencil outlines.

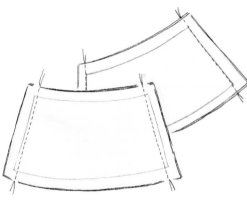

3 For the outer casing machine stitch two panels of lining fabric together down the sides, right sides facing, and following the pencil lines exactly. Repeat for the inner casing but reduce the width between the pencil markings by 3 mm (⅛ in) at each side for a tight fit.

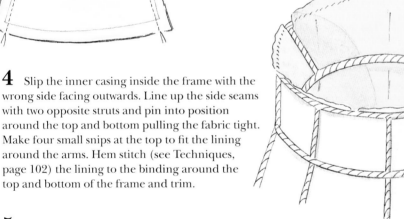

4 Slip the inner casing inside the frame with the wrong side facing outwards. Line up the side seams with two opposite struts and pin into position around the top and bottom pulling the fabric tight. Make four small snips at the top to fit the lining around the arms. Hem stitch (see Techniques, page 102) the lining to the binding around the top and bottom of the frame and trim.

5 Slip the outer lining casing over the top of the shade, aligning the seams with those on the inner casing. Pin and hem stitch in place, top and bottom.

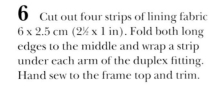

6 Cut out four strips of lining fabric 6 x 2.5 cm (2½ x 1 in). Fold both long edges to the middle and wrap a strip under each arm of the duplex fitting. Hand sew to the frame top and trim.

7 To hide the raw edges cut a strip of lining fabric 82.5 x 2.5 cm (33 x 1in) for the bottom and 55 x 2.5 cm (22 x 1 in) for the top. On both strips fold the long edges to the middle and press. Pin then slip stitch (see Techniques, page 102) the strips in place along both folded edges, tucking under the raw ends.

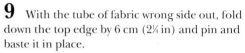

8 For the smocked skirt cut a piece of Provençal cotton 45 x 128 cm (18 x 51 in). Fold it in half matching the short ends, right sides facing and pin and machine stitch together, using a 1 cm (½ in) seam allowance. Press open the seam.

9 With the tube of fabric wrong side out, fold down the top edge by 6 cm (2¼ in) and pin and baste it in place.

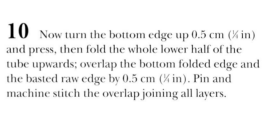

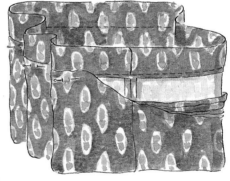

10 Now turn the bottom edge up 0.5 cm (¼ in) and press, then fold the whole lower half of the tube upwards; overlap the bottom folded edge and the basted raw edge by 0.5 cm (¼ in). Pin and machine stitch the overlap joining all layers.

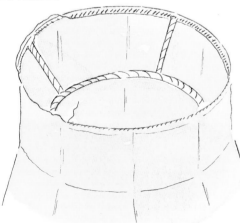

11 Machine three parallel lines of stitches 1¼ cm (½in) down from the top edge and 1¼ cm (½in) apart all round the top of the cover. Unpick three holes on the side seam made in step 8. Insert one 48 cm (19 in) length of elastic into each hole, threading them through with a safety pin. Pull the elastic through and hand sew one end over the other with a 1 cm (½ in) overlap. Slip stitch the openings closed, turn the cover inside out and fit over the shade.

covered shade

This cloche hat shade is made from a pink silk taffeta and trimmed with cream silk and a hand-made rosette at the top. The heavily gathered effect all round the shade is achieved by a series of narrow, even knife pleats at the top, stretching down to meet the tightly gathered bottom circumference. Because the shade is covered over the top it is vital to use a very low-watt bulb positioned well below the covering, to minimize the risk of scorching.

materials & equipment

frame with six side struts, six top struts and reverse gimbal fitting: 24 cm (9½ in) diameter bottom; 15 cm (6 in) diameter top; 4 cm (1½ in) diameter centre ring; 14 cm (5½ in) height

125 cm (50 in) pink silk taffeta, 115 cm (45 in) wide

25 cm (10 in) lining fabric, 115 cm (45 in) wide

50 cm (20 in) cream silk, 115 cm (45 in) wide

basic sewing kit (see page 98)

1 Start by binding the top and bottom rings of the frame with binding tape (see Techniques, page 101).

2 Cut out two pieces of pink silk taffeta 114 x 17 cm (45 x 6½ in). Mark each into three equal sections with small snips adding an extra 1 cm (½ in) seam allowance at the sides.

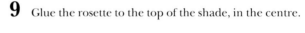

3 Sew two narrow lines of running stitches along the bottom edges before pinning a series of narrow even knife pleats along the top of each, to fit the two halves of the circumference of the top frame. Baste them in place.

4 Pin one piece to half of the frame along the top, matching the marks with the side struts. Pull the gathers to fit the bottom and pin in the same way. Repeat for the other half, turning in and overlapping the side seams. Hem stitch (see Techniques, page 102) the top and bottom edges and trim.

5 Cut a piece of lining fabric 17 x 75 cm (6½ x 30 in) and mark into six equal sections as in step 2. Pin the marks to the side struts on the inside, folding in 1 cm (½ in) at one end to overlap the other. Pin between the struts making a few small pleats along the top edge and cutting the fabric to fit around the top struts and gimbal arms. Hem stitch to the top and bottom rings and trim.

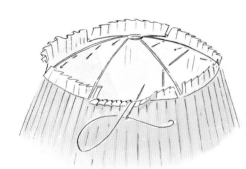

6 Cut out a circle of lining fabric 20 cm (8 in) in diameter (see Techniques, page 98) and place it over the top of the frame. Pin and hem stitch to the top ring and trim.

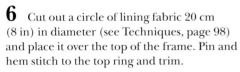

7 For the top outer covering cut a circle of silk taffeta 23 cm (9 in) in diameter, cutting a second circle from the middle with a 5 cm (2 in) diameter. Sew circles of running stitches close to the edge of the inner circle and around the outer edge, and pull the inner circle tightly into gathers, securing them in place with a few stitches. Pull the outer row of gathers to fit the top ring. Pin and hem stitch the circle to the top ring.

8 For the rosette, cut a strip of taffeta 4 x 22 cm (1½ x 8½ in) and with right sides facing machine stitch the short ends together using a 0.5 cm (¼ in) seam allowance. Fold in half lengthways, wrong sides facing and sew a circle of running stitches close to the top raw edges; pull tightly to gather the centre.

9 Glue the rosette to the top of the shade, in the centre.

10 To neaten the top edge, cut two strips of taffeta on the bias, one pink and one cream, each measuring 51 x 4 cm (20½ x 1½ in). Machine stitch the short ends on each, right sides together with diagonal seams and a 1 cm (½ in) seam allowance. Turn up one long edge to the wrong side by 1 cm (½ in) and press.

11 To attach, lay the right side of the cream binding against the wrong side of the pink. Pin the raw edges to the frame, pink side down, and with the binding sitting on the inside. Hem stitch in place.

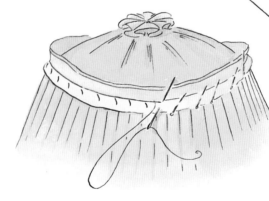

12 Run a line of glue around the top edge, fold the turned edge of the cream binding onto it and repeat for the pink strip; make sure a circle of cream remains visible.

13 Repeat steps 11 and 12 for the bottom edge using 75 x 4 cm (30 x 1½ in) strips.

scalloped crown

This unusual shade is made from a single piece of lilac and white checked cotton stiffened with iron-on interfacing to allow it to stand upright yet remain loosely attached to the frame. The scallops are made in a curve along the bottom edge so the brim is deeper at the front and gradually slopes down as it meets the seam at the back. If the mathematics of the scallops puts you off, simply straighten the top edge and have a plain smoothly curving brim.

materials & equipment

frame with four struts and a base fitting: 15 cm (6 in) diameter bottom ring; 7.5 cm (3 in) diameter top ring; 30 cm (12 in) height

75 cm (30 in) lilac and white checked reversible cotton, 115 cm (45 in) wide

50 cm (20 in) medium weight iron-on interfacing

1 cm (½ in) wide binding tape

50 cm (20 in) square card for template

1 Bind the entire frame (see Techniques, page 101).

2 For the template draw a vertical line measuring 30 cm (12 in), and a horizontal one across its base with 25 cm (10 in) on either side of the vertical. At the top of the vertical line draw another horizontal line extending for 15 cm (6 in) on either side. Join up the sides. At point A, pin a piece of string with a pencil attached and draw an arc from B to C. Draw a second arc 2.5 cm (1 in) below the first one. Place a piece of string along the first arc and measure and mark it into twelve equal sections. Carefully draw twelve scallops between the marks with the top of each scallop meeting the outer arc. For the scallops along the top divide the top line into six equal sections then draw a horizontal line 2.5 cm (1 in) above it; use the marks to draw six scallops as before.

3 Use the template to cut out the pattern with the check fabric on the bias (see Techniques, page 103). Mark the widest horizontal line across the fabric very lightly with a pencil on both sides.

4 With the fabric wrong side up, cut a piece of iron-on interfacing slightly larger all round than the upper portion of the pattern, aligning a straight edge of interfacing along the pencil line. Iron on the interfacing and trim off the excess around the sides and top edge.

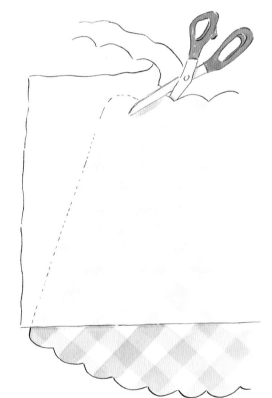

5 Turn the fabric over so it is right side up and cut a piece of iron-on interfacing slightly larger all round than the portion below the line. Align a straight edge of interfacing 1 cm (⅛ in) below the line. Iron on the interfacing and trim away the excess around the sides and bottom scalloped edge.

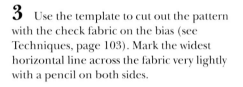

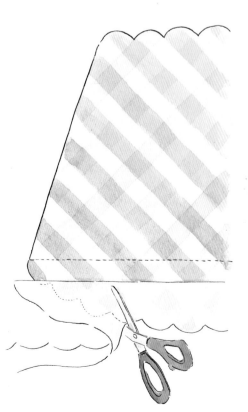

6 With the fabric wrong side up once again, work a narrow zigzag along the curved edges of the bottom scallops using a contrasting burgundy thread. This will neaten, strengthen and decorate the raw edges.

7 Flip the fabric to the right side again and work the same zigzag along the curved edges of the top scallops and down the right-hand side.

8 Turn up the lower portion of the shade by making a fold along the lower line of interfacing. Run a line of fabric adhesive down the outside edge of the plain side and press it onto the inside of the opposite edge, thus forming a hat shape.

9 Slip the shade over the frame. To prevent the loose-fitting shade from slipping off the frame make tiny stab stitches at three points spaced around the top and bottom rings of the frame, taking the needle through both the fabric and the binding.

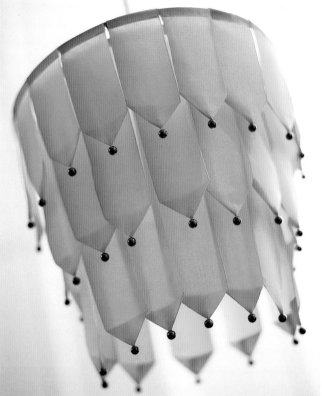

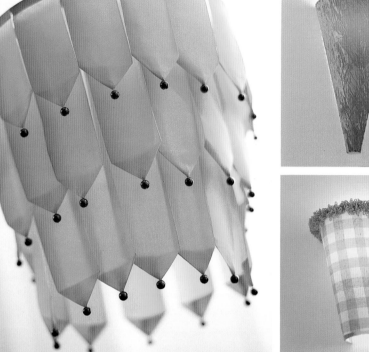

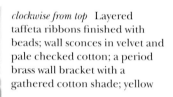

clockwise from top Layered taffeta ribbons finished with beads; wall sconces in velvet and pale checked cotton; a period brass wall bracket with a gathered cotton shade; yellow laminated hessian on a pendant drum shade; metal eyelets with rings attach a loose shade to a circular frame; pretty printed floaty voile is gathered tightly on a collared pendant.

Thin yellow cotton was dipped in fabric stiffener and then draped over a panelled shade. The moulded shape was then finished with a satin tassel.

This fun harlequin chandelier was knitted from fine yellow silk and draped over a ring frame. Gilt coins catch the light and keep the shade in shape.

A tightly knitted pagoda-shaped pendant, stretched over a series of ring frames, makes a most effective and clever overhead light fixture.

wall and ceiling lamps

Ceiling lights tend to operate as main sources of light, often illuminating a whole room. Although they should be capable of casting plenty of light they should also be a decorative feature and draw the eye upwards. Wall lights come as uplights, bracket lights and sconces and are useful for throwing light onto surrounding surfaces that reflect back into the room.

above Thin grey and cream striped voile is tightly gathered to form a dense cover on a circular wall shield, which curves gently to hide the bulb from view on each side. A flame retardant lining is used to prevent scorching.
left A wall sconce throws light in a wide arc up to the ceiling, and creates a wonder-fully subtle effect. This one is laminated with rich yellow crushed velvet and edged with a laced leather thong.

linen
loose cover

An ornate wall sconce is topped with a piece of the palest apricot linen no bigger than a pocket handkerchief. The soft-hued fabric sits loosely on a card shade and looks as if it has just floated down and settled in place creating a gentle pool of background light, for a relaxed atmosphere.

materials & equipment

card undershade with bulb fitting: 8 cm (3 in) diameter top; 18 cm (7 in) diameter bottom; 13 cm (5 ¼ in) height

50 cm (20 in) apricot linen, 115 cm (45 in) wide

pattern paper

compass, or pencil, drawing pin and string

basic sewing kit (see page 98)

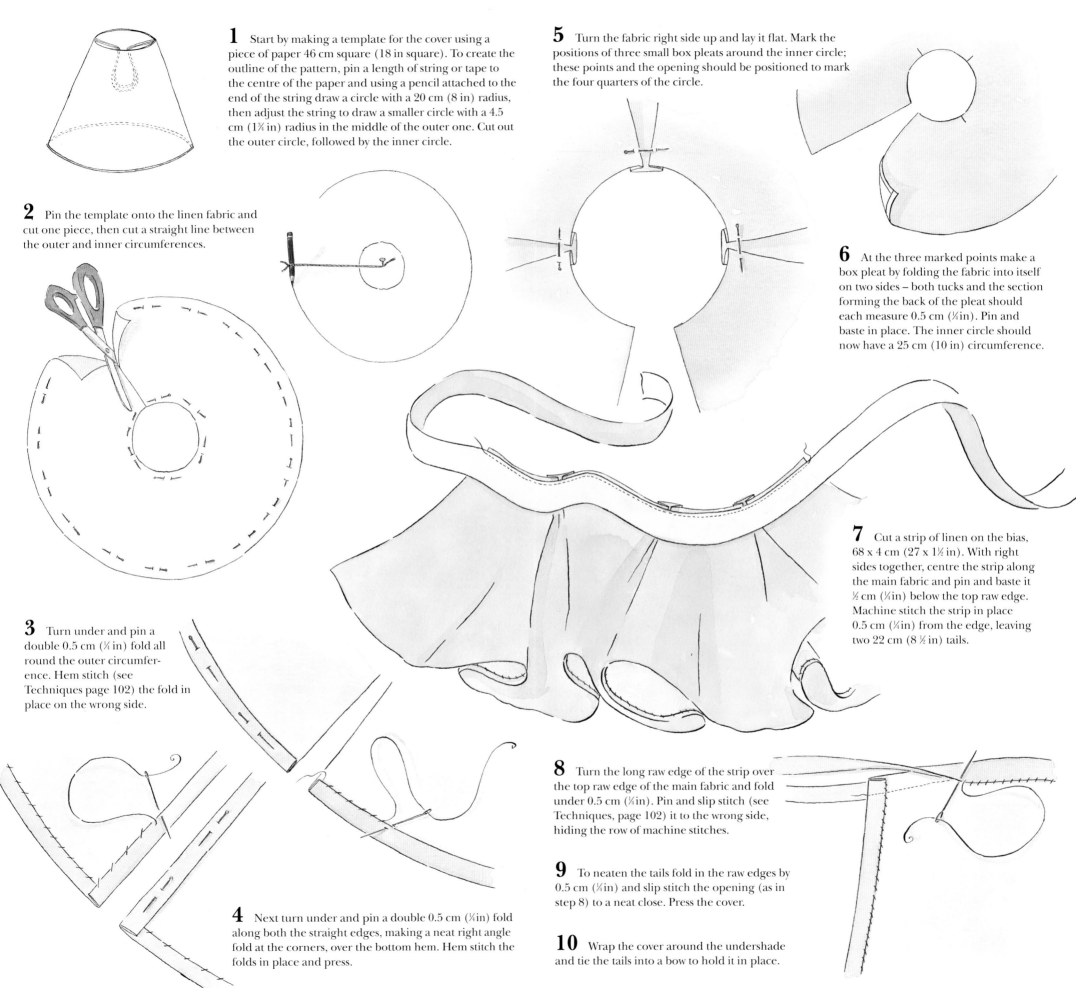

1 Start by making a template for the cover using a piece of paper 46 cm square (18 in square). To create the outline of the pattern, pin a length of string or tape to the centre of the paper and using a pencil attached to the end of the string draw a circle with a 20 cm (8 in) radius, then adjust the string to draw a smaller circle with a 4.5 cm (1¾ in) radius in the middle of the outer one. Cut out the outer circle, followed by the inner circle.

2 Pin the template onto the linen fabric and cut one piece, then cut a straight line between the outer and inner circumferences.

3 Turn under and pin a double 0.5 cm (⅛ in) fold all round the outer circumference. Hem stitch (see Techniques page 102) the fold in place on the wrong side.

4 Next turn under and pin a double 0.5 cm (⅛ in) fold along both the straight edges, making a neat right angle fold at the corners, over the bottom hem. Hem stitch the folds in place and press.

5 Turn the fabric right side up and lay it flat. Mark the positions of three small box pleats around the inner circle; these points and the opening should be positioned to mark the four quarters of the circle.

6 At the three marked points make a box pleat by folding the fabric into itself on two sides – both tucks and the section forming the back of the pleat should each measure 0.5 cm (⅛ in). Pin and baste in place. The inner circle should now have a 25 cm (10 in) circumference.

7 Cut a strip of linen on the bias, 68 x 4 cm (27 x 1½ in). With right sides together, centre the strip along the main fabric and pin and baste it ½ cm (⅛ in) below the top raw edge. Machine stitch the strip in place 0.5 cm (⅛ in) from the edge, leaving two 22 cm (8 ½ in) tails.

8 Turn the long raw edge of the strip over the top raw edge of the main fabric and fold under 0.5 cm (⅛ in). Pin and slip stitch (see Techniques, page 102) it to the wrong side, hiding the row of machine stitches.

9 To neaten the tails fold in the raw edges by 0.5 cm (⅛ in) and slip stitch the opening (as in step 8) to a neat close. Press the cover.

10 Wrap the cover around the undershade and tie the tails into a bow to hold it in place.

gingham in gathers

For a lampshade like this miniature square, a small-scale pattern such as gingham is ideal. To give the tiny shade a little more impact the gingham has been very tightly gathered all round the top and bottom and a matching braid has been attached to neaten the edges and add a decorative touch.

materials & equipment

square frame with four side struts and clip fitting: 9 cm (3½ in) square top;
13 cm (5 in) square bottom; 10 cm (4 in) height

50 cm (20 in) blue and white gingham, 115 cm (45 in) wide

50 cm (20 in) white silk lampshade lining, 115 cm (45 in) wide

1 cm (½ in) wide binding tape

100 cm (40 in) decorative braid

fabric adhesive

basic sewing kit (see page 98)

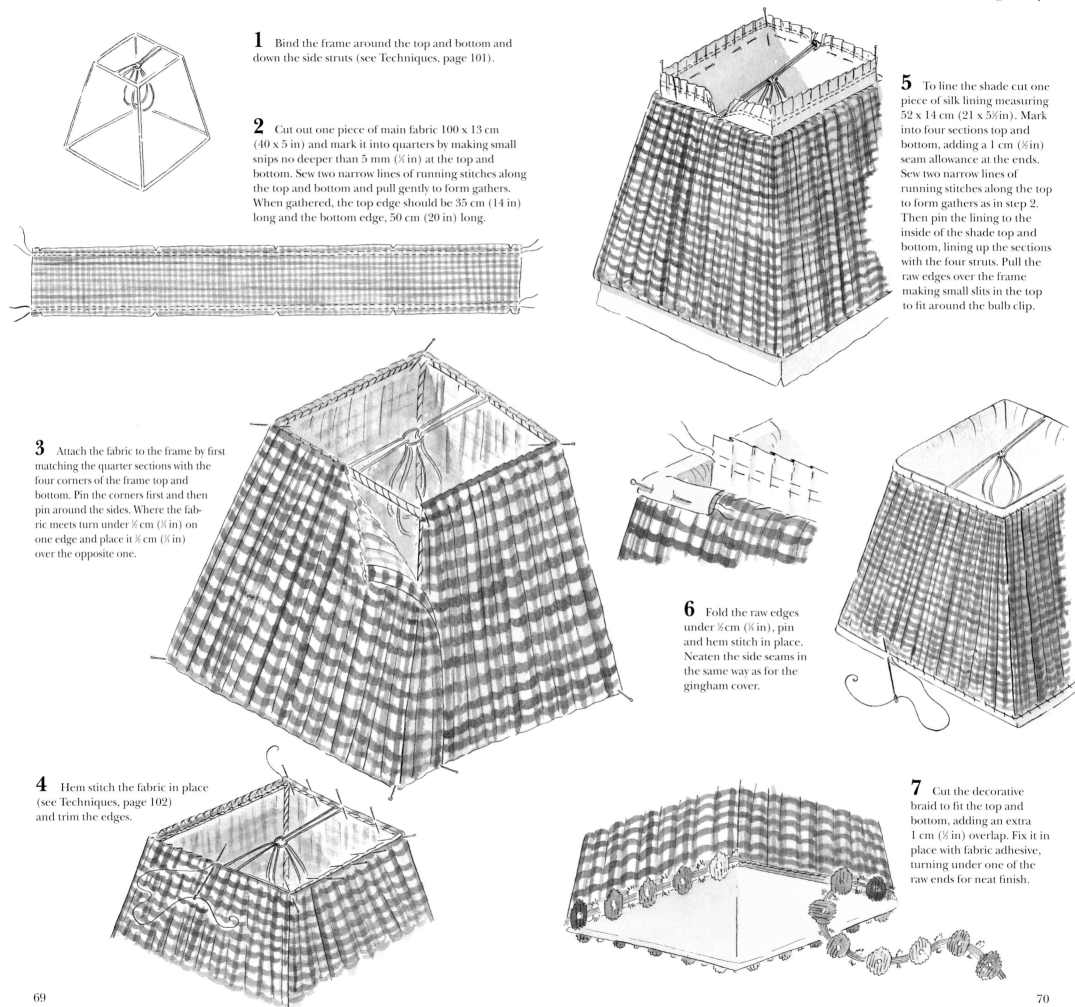

1 Bind the frame around the top and bottom and down the side struts (see Techniques, page 101).

2 Cut out one piece of main fabric 100 x 13 cm (40 x 5 in) and mark it into quarters by making small snips no deeper than 5 mm (⅛ in) at the top and bottom. Sew two narrow lines of running stitches along the top and bottom and pull gently to form gathers. When gathered, the top edge should be 35 cm (14 in) long and the bottom edge, 50 cm (20 in) long.

5 To line the shade cut one piece of silk lining measuring 52 x 14 cm (21 x 5½ in). Mark into four sections top and bottom, adding a 1 cm (½ in) seam allowance at the ends. Sew two narrow lines of running stitches along the top to form gathers as in step 2. Then pin the lining to the inside of the shade top and bottom, lining up the sections with the four struts. Pull the raw edges over the frame making small slits in the top to fit around the bulb clip.

3 Attach the fabric to the frame by first matching the quarter sections with the four corners of the frame top and bottom. Pin the corners first and then pin around the sides. Where the fabric meets turn under ½ cm (⅛ in) on one edge and place it ½ cm (⅛ in) over the opposite one.

6 Fold the raw edges under ½ cm (⅛ in), pin and hem stitch in place. Neaten the side seams in the same way as for the gingham cover.

4 Hem stitch the fabric in place (see Techniques, page 102) and trim the edges.

7 Cut the decorative braid to fit the top and bottom, adding an extra 1 cm (½ in) overlap. Fix it in place with fabric adhesive, turning under one of the raw ends for neat finish.

chandelier candle shades

Six miniature cones with pretty scalloped edges are made from laminated yellow gingham; here, the tiny checks ensure that there is an even distribution of light through the shade. Using a template the shades are quick and easy to make and each one sits neatly on a bulb clip on each arm of a chandelier.

materials & equipment

5 cm (2 in) diameter bulb clip: 5 cm (2 in) diameter top; 13 cm (5 in) diameter bottom; 10 cm (4 in) height

17 x 35 cm (7 x 14 in) yellow cotton gingham for each shade

17 x 35 cm (7 x 14 in) self-adhesive backing for each shade

clothes pegs

basic sewing kit (see page 98)

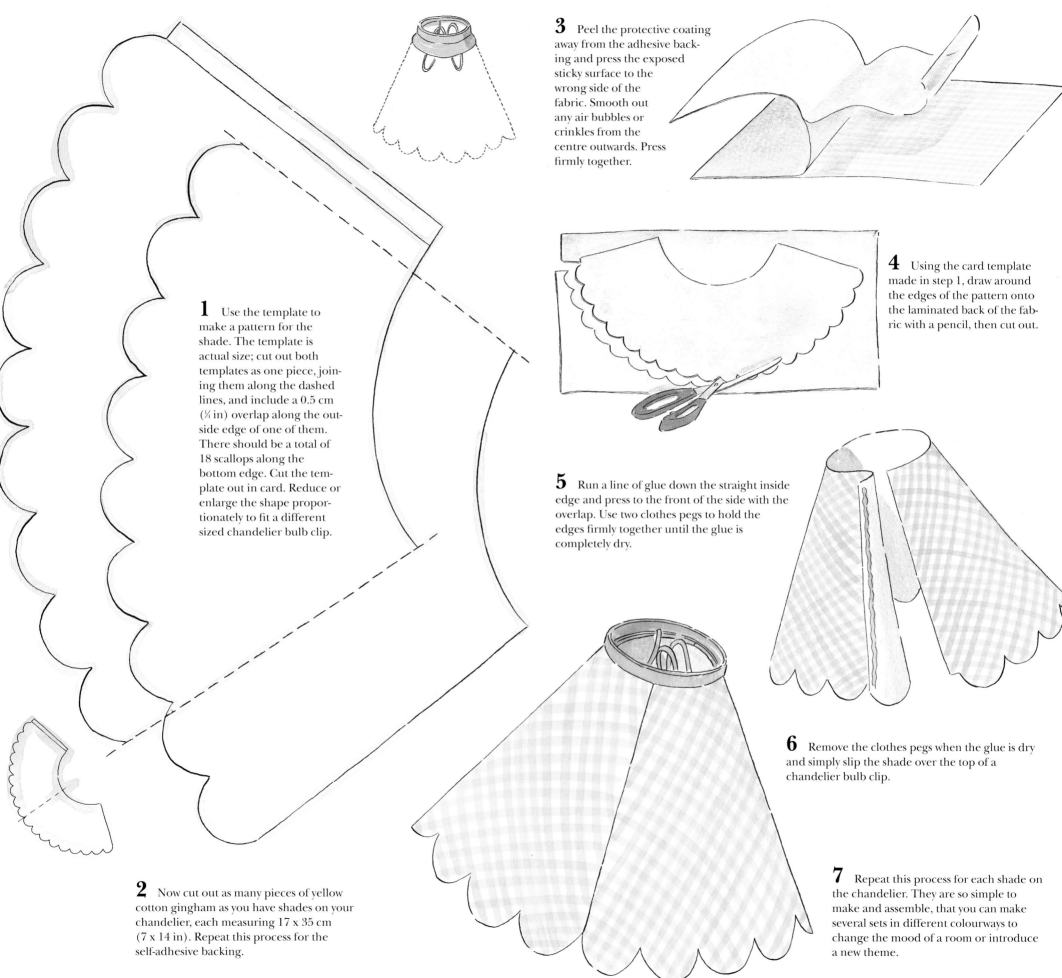

3 Peel the protective coating away from the adhesive backing and press the exposed sticky surface to the wrong side of the fabric. Smooth out any air bubbles or crinkles from the centre outwards. Press firmly together.

1 Use the template to make a pattern for the shade. The template is actual size; cut out both templates as one piece, joining them along the dashed lines, and include a 0.5 cm (⅛ in) overlap along the outside edge of one of them. There should be a total of 18 scallops along the bottom edge. Cut the template out in card. Reduce or enlarge the shape proportionately to fit a different sized chandelier bulb clip.

4 Using the card template made in step 1, draw around the edges of the pattern onto the laminated back of the fabric with a pencil, then cut out.

5 Run a line of glue down the straight inside edge and press to the front of the side with the overlap. Use two clothes pegs to hold the edges firmly together until the glue is completely dry.

6 Remove the clothes pegs when the glue is dry and simply slip the shade over the top of a chandelier bulb clip.

2 Now cut out as many pieces of yellow cotton gingham as you have shades on your chandelier, each measuring 17 x 35 cm (7 x 14 in). Repeat this process for the self-adhesive backing.

7 Repeat this process for each shade on the chandelier. They are so simple to make and assemble, that you can make several sets in different colourways to change the mood of a room or introduce a new theme.

two-tiered hanging lamp

This exquisite ceiling lamp is perfect for hanging over a kitchen or dining room table. It is a Swedish design and consists of a pretty cotton print tailored around a cone-shaped frame and an outer ring covered by a deep gathered frill that hangs down giving an original two-tiered effect.

materials & equipment

frame with six side struts and brass ceiling gimbal mechanism: 8 cm (3 in) diameter top; 35 cm (14 in) diameter bottom; 23 cm (9 in) height; four 8 cm (3 in) arms join 43 cm (17 in) diameter outer bottom ring

75 cm (30 in) lining fabric, 115 cm (45 in) wide

125 cm (50 in) red and white cotton print, 150 cm (60 in) wide

basic sewing kit (see page 98)

1 Bind the top and both the inner and outer bottom rings of the frame with binding tape (see Techniques, page 101).

7 To neaten the bottom of the inner ring (the top ring will be covered by a brass fitting) cut a strip of main fabric 4 x 108 cm (1 ½ x 43 in). Fold both long edges to the wrong side by 0.5 cm (¼ in) and press. Pin and slip stitch (see Techniques, page 102) in place around the upper and lower edges of the binding, tucking in the ends to hide the raw edges. Make tiny slits in the strip to fit the arms.

2 Cut two pieces of lining fabric, 28 x 59 cm (11 x 23 in). Pin one piece to half of the frame on the outside, top and bottom, adjusting the pins as you pull the fabric tight. Mark the outline of the pins with a pencil to show the seam lines, before removing them.

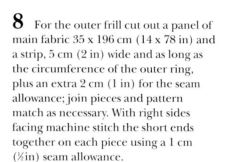

8 For the outer frill cut out a panel of main fabric 35 x 196 cm (14 x 78 in) and a strip, 5 cm (2 in) wide and as long as the circumference of the outer ring, plus an extra 2 cm (1 in) for the seam allowance; join pieces and pattern match as necessary. With right sides facing machine stitch the short ends together on each piece using a 1 cm (½ in) seam allowance.

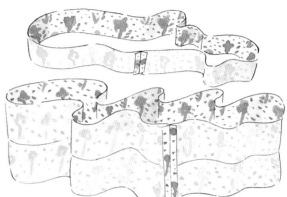

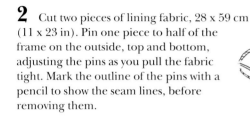

3 Pin the second piece of lining to the pencil-marked one, right sides facing. Baste along the pencil lines at the side, but reduce the width at the 'waist' by 5 mm (¼ in) on each side, for a tight fit. Machine two narrow lines of stitching down both curved edges, following the basting stitches and trim the excess fabric.

9 Fold the main fabric in half matching raw edges with wrong sides facing and sew two narrow lines of running stitches 1 cm (½ in) from the top raw edge. Pull the threads into even gathers to fit the circumference of the outer ring. Using a 1 cm (½ in) seam allowance, pin and machine stitch the fabric to the strip, right sides facing and matching raw edges.

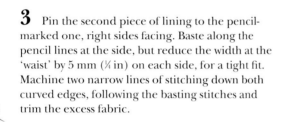

4 Slip the lining casing inside the frame with the seam allowances facing outwards and the seams aligned with side struts. Pin to the top and bottom rings of the frame so the fabric is tight. Hem stitch (see Techniques, page 102) to the binding tape and trim.

5 Cut out a panel of main fabric 150 x 28 cm (60 x 11 in), joining pieces together and pattern matching as necessary. Mark into six equal sections top and bottom with small snips, leaving a 1 cm (½ in) seam allowance at each short end.

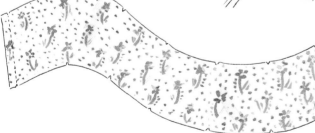

6 Begin by pinning the marks to the six side struts top and bottom, turning in and overlapping one raw end 1 cm (½ in) over the other. Pin a series of even knife pleats between the marks along the top, until the fabric fits the ring exactly. Fan the pleats out evenly and pin around the bottom edge. Hem stitch the top and bottom of the cover and trim.

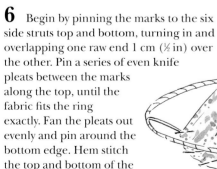

10 Place the frill around the outer ring, wrapping the wrong side of the strip over the frame. Tuck under the raw edge on the strip, make slits to fit the arms and pin and slip stitch it to the underside of the bound frame.

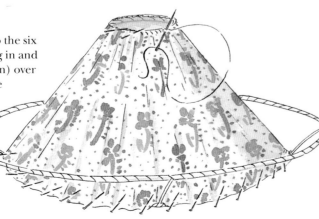

striped
wall shield

This minute half shade is designed to shield a bulb on a wall sconce.
The unusual shape is ideal for elaborate and ornate sconces. The
striped silk taffeta is stretched very tightly around the frame and the
same stripe is cut on the bias to trim the edges. The whole project is
made with hand stitching only.

materials & equipment

*half cylinder frame with bulb clip fitting: 16 cm (6¼ in) wide; 13 cm (5 in)
height at centre; 11 cm (4¼ in) height at sides*

75 cm (30 in) striped silk taffeta, 115 cm (45 in) wide

25 cm (10 in) lining fabric, 115 cm (45 in) wide

basic sewing kit (see page 98)

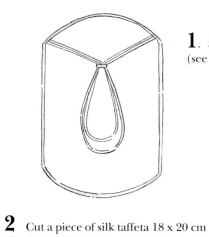

1. Start by binding all round the frame with binding tape (see Techniques, page 101).

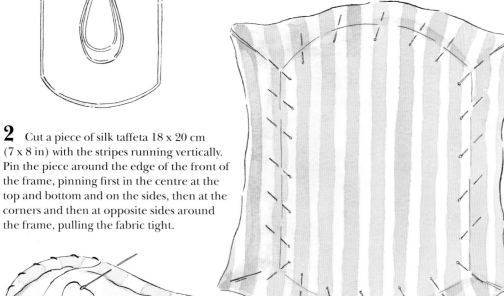

2 Cut a piece of silk taffeta 18 x 20 cm (7 x 8 in) with the stripes running vertically. Pin the piece around the edge of the front of the frame, pinning first in the centre at the top and bottom and on the sides, then at the corners and then at opposite sides around the frame, pulling the fabric tight.

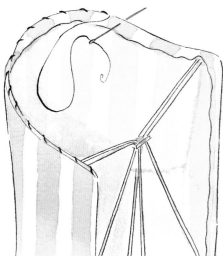

3 Hem stitch (see Techniques, page 102) to the binding all round the frame and trim.

4 Next cut out a 20 x 18 cm (8 x 7 in) piece of lining. Pin it around the edge of the reverse side of the frame in the same way as for the silk taffeta, overlapping the raw edge of the silk taffeta. Cut slits to fit the fabric around the arms for the bulb clip.

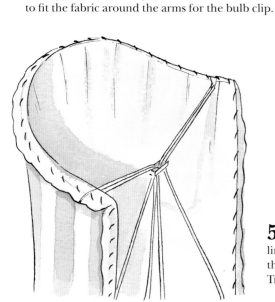

5 Once the pins are in position and the lining is really tight, hem stitch the lining to the binding all round the inside of the frame. Trim away the excess fabric.

6 To hide the joins where the arms of the bulb clip meet the top of the frame, cut out two strips of lining 5 x 2.5 cm (2 x 1 in). Fold the long edges of each strip to the centre and press. Wrap a strip round each join then pin and hand sew the ends of the strip to the frame. Trim away the excess.

7 Cut a strip of silk taffeta on the bias (see Techniques, page 103) so that the stripes run diagonally, 55 x 2 cm (21¼ x 1 in). Fold in 0.5 cm (¼ in) along both long edges and press flat.

8 Pin the bias binding around the perimeter of the frame to hide the raw edges, positioning the upper edge along the top. Start and end in a corner, turning under one raw edge to overlap the other; form neat tucks at the remaining corners where the fabric bunches.

9 Slip stitch in place (see Techniques, page 102), along both folded edges so that the stitches are almost invisible.

floor lamps

By their nature floor lamps tend to be more prominent than their counterparts found on walls, tables and mantelpieces or shelves. Because they are free-standing and relatively tall, whether a traditional standard lamp or a lower swan-neck reading light, they require a shade that is in keeping with the height and shape of the stand.

above, from left A large boxed Empire shade looks handsome on a huge column base: a lesser shade would be dwarfed by such an impressive base. A modern metal base supports a more traditional box-pleated Empire shade, made from a striped cotton – the wide openings at the top and base of the shade allow plenty of light to shine out. A tall narrow shape is ideal for a room where a floor lamp is the best solution, but space is limited; this cone is covered in crushed silk, and sits on a simple metal pole. This cream silk square banded shade is gently waisted for an elegant feel.

right, from left A bi-coloured silk with wide stripes is cut out on the bias and simply laminated onto a conical shade. A filmy white fabric skirted shade sits atop a thin tripod base by Philip Starck. A pale aqua *toile de Jouy* fabric, knife pleated and finished with a gathered ruffle, covers the shade on a swing-armed standard lamp. A huge carved wooden base needs a proportionately large shade – this one is octagonal and covered in a pale check neatly mitred at the seams. Tall and elegant, this cone-topped stand with a three-pronged base would fit well into a modern setting.

stripes round
a drum

A drum is a traditional shape for standard lamps and the open top and
bottom throw out plenty of light. Here the shade is simply a cylinder of
laminated striped fabric. The formal stripes and stiff
surface have been softened with ready-made double
bobble fringing.

materials & equipment

40 cm (16 in) diameter plain wire ring

40 cm (16 in) diameter gimbal wire ring

50 cm (20 in) striped cotton, 115 cm (45 in) wide

1 cm (½ in) wide binding tape

135 cm (4½ ft) single bobble fringe

135 cm (4½ ft) double bobble fringe

150 cm (60 in) self-adhesive lampshade backing, 115 cm (45 in) wide

fabric adhesive

clothes pegs

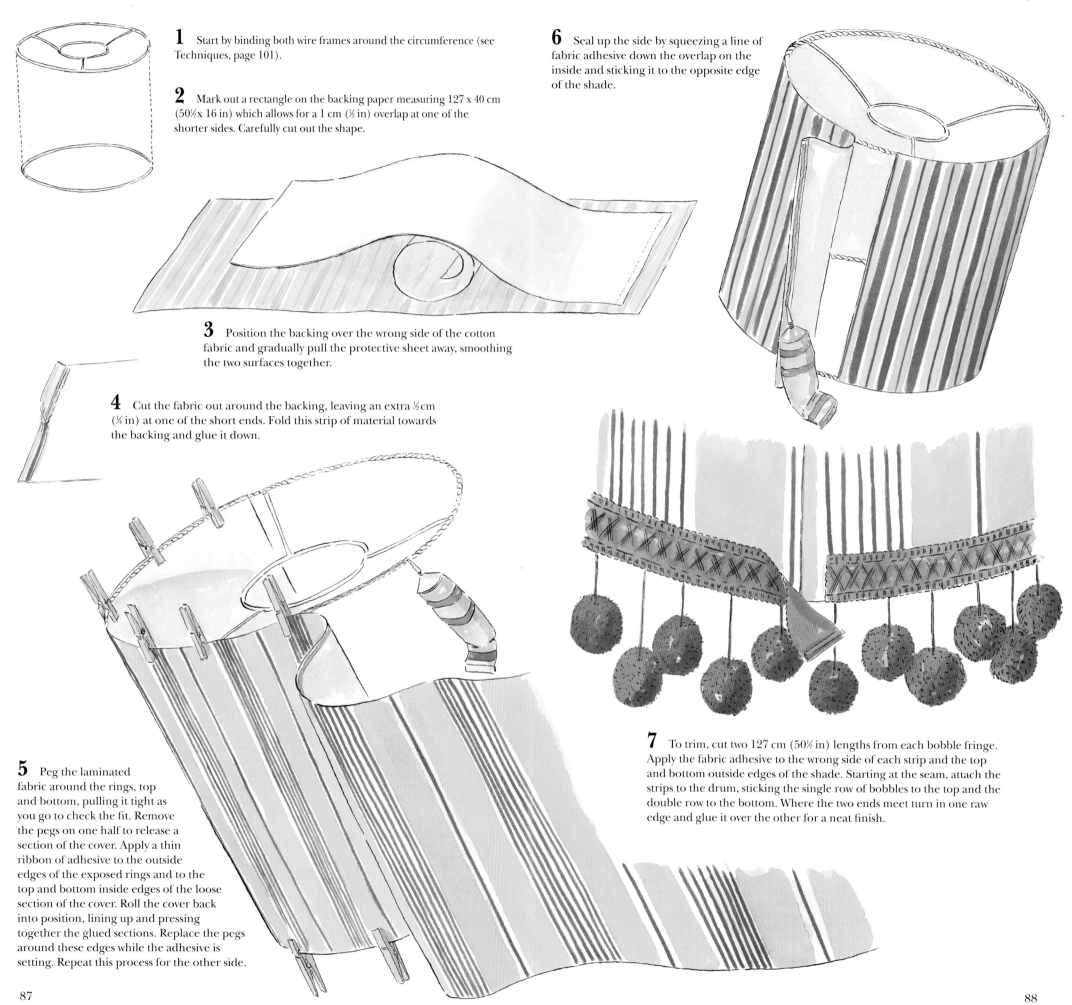

1 Start by binding both wire frames around the circumference (see Techniques, page 101).

2 Mark out a rectangle on the backing paper measuring 127 x 40 cm (50½ x 16 in) which allows for a 1 cm (½ in) overlap at one of the shorter sides. Carefully cut out the shape.

3 Position the backing over the wrong side of the cotton fabric and gradually pull the protective sheet away, smoothing the two surfaces together.

4 Cut the fabric out around the backing, leaving an extra ½ cm (¼ in) at one of the short ends. Fold this strip of material towards the backing and glue it down.

5 Peg the laminated fabric around the rings, top and bottom, pulling it tight as you go to check the fit. Remove the pegs on one half to release a section of the cover. Apply a thin ribbon of adhesive to the outside edges of the exposed rings and to the top and bottom inside edges of the loose section of the cover. Roll the cover back into position, lining up and pressing together the glued sections. Replace the pegs around these edges while the adhesive is setting. Repeat this process for the other side.

6 Seal up the side by squeezing a line of fabric adhesive down the overlap on the inside and sticking it to the opposite edge of the shade.

7 To trim, cut two 127 cm (50½ in) lengths from each bobble fringe. Apply the fabric adhesive to the wrong side of each strip and the top and bottom outside edges of the shade. Starting at the seam, attach the strips to the drum, sticking the single row of bobbles to the top and the double row to the bottom. Where the two ends meet turn in one raw edge and glue it over the other for a neat finish.

leather-stitched chimney

Vivid blue linen is laminated to stiffen it and then cut and rolled into a tall cone or chimney shape. Because of the lamination the fabric can be punched with holes so that a black leather thong can be threaded through it to secure the sides, creating an unusual fastening and trim.

material & equipment

10 cm (4 in) diameter plain wire ring

25 cm (10 in) diameter base fitting gimbal

100 cm (40 in) blue canvas, 115 cm (45 in) wide

1 cm (½ in) wide black binding tape

300 cm (120 in) leather thong

75 cm (30 in) square thin card

100 cm (40 in) self-adhesive lampshade backing, 115 cm (45 in) wide

multi-purpose glue and clothes pegs

six-way hole punch

90

1 First bind the smaller ring and the outside edge and struts of the base gimbal ring (see Techniques, page 101).

2 Take the sheet of card and starting in the bottom right-hand corner mark a horizontal line equal to the 28 cm (10 in) diameter of the bottom ring (A). Draw a vertical line upwards through the middle of the horizontal one and mark a point 35 cm (14 in), equal to the height of the shade, above the first one (B). Centre a second horizontal line through this point 10 cm (4 in) long, or equal to the diameter of the top ring (C). Draw in the sides of the shade, continuing the lines until they meet.

To create the outline of the pattern, pin a length of string to the tip of the triangle and using a pencil attached to the end of the string draw two arcs; start one at the top right-hand corner of the shade shape and the other at the bottom right-hand corner. The arcs should be as long as the circumference of the top and bottom of the shade plus 1 cm (½ in) overlap.

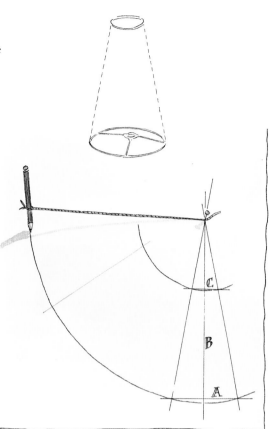

3 Cut out the template and place it over the lampshade backing. Mark the outline of the template and cut out one piece.

4 Position the backing over the wrong side of the fabric on the cross grain and adhere the two together by peeling back the protective sheet.

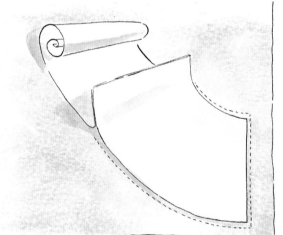

5 Cut out the fabric around the backing adding an extra 1 cm (½ in) overlap all the way round, cutting a triangle of fabric away at each corner to reduce the bulk. Drizzle a line of glue along the wrong side of this overlap, fold it over and stick it to the backing.

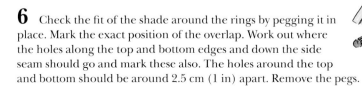

6 Check the fit of the shade around the rings by pegging it in place. Mark the exact position of the overlap. Work out where the holes along the top and bottom edges and down the side seam should go and mark these also. The holes around the top and bottom should be around 2.5 cm (1 in) apart. Remove the pegs.

7 Now punch holes through the pencil marks using a six-way punch.

8 To assemble the shade run a line of glue around the top and bottom inside edges of the cone and around the outside edges of both rings. Roll the shade onto the rings, lining up the strips of glue and place pegs around the edges to hold the rings in position. Remove the pegs when the glue is dry.

9 Snip the leather thong into a point at one end and thread it through the holes on the side seam. Start at the top, leaving about 25 cm (10 in) of thong hanging. Thread down and then back up to form the crosses. Trim to 25 cm (10 in) and tie the two loose ends into a bow to finish. Then thread the thong around the top and bottom edges, overlapping the rim. Knot the ends to secure.

pleated
cone with collar

This frame has a distinctive profile, characterized by its elegant collar
at the top. The design contributes to the smart look of a
lampshade made up in formal pleats, which are pulled in at the neck
by a decorative binding and emphasized by the cream
and olive striped taffeta.

materials & equipment

frame with six struts and drop pendant fitting: 15 cm (6 in) diameter top;
25 cm (10 in) diameter bottom; 20 cm (8in) height including
3 cm (1¼ in) collar

25 cm (10 in) lining fabric, 115 cm (45 in) wide

100 cm (40 in) narrow striped taffeta, 115 cm (45 in) wide

1 cm (½ in) wide binding tape

fabric adhesive

basic sewing kit (see page 98)

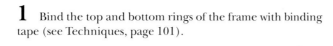

1 Bind the top and bottom rings of the frame with binding tape (see Techniques, page 101).

2 To line the shade, cut a piece of lining fabric 83 x 23 cm (32½ x 9 in). Sew two narrow lines of running stitches along the top edge and pull them into gathers so the top edge fits the inner circumference of the frame top, plus an extra 1 cm (½ in) overlap at each end.

3 Pin the lining evenly inside the top ring, making three small snips to accommodate the pendant arms. Then turn in one raw edge by 1 cm (½ in) to overlap the other and pin the bottom edge in place. Hem stitch (see Techniques, page 102) to secure the lining top and bottom and trim.

4 Cut two panels of striped taffeta measuring 23 x 115 cm (9 x 45 in). Each panel must be pleated to fit half the circumference of the shade with a 1 cm (½ in) overlap at each short end. Pleat the top edge first where the pleats are tighter, and begin each one on the edge of a stripe; make sure they are all equal in width and pin as you go.

5 Pin one pleated panel to half of the top of the frame by removing a pin at a time and re-securing it through the pleat and binding. To form the pleats at the bottom, pull the fabric down parallel to the side struts, following the edge of a stripe from a top pleat and pin even pleats around the base, allowing them to fan out. Repeat this process for the other panel on the second half, folding under the raw edges and overlapping the panels where they meet.

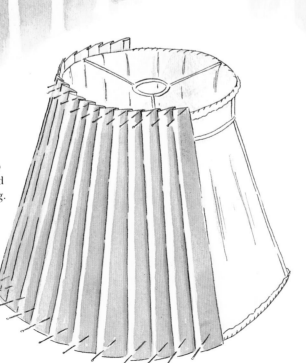

6 Hem stitch top and bottom pleats in place and trim.

7 Cut a strip of taffeta 52 x 3 cm (20½ x 1½ in) on the bias. Match up the stripes and machine stitch the ends, right sides together with a diagonal seam, using a 1 cm (½ in) seam allowance.

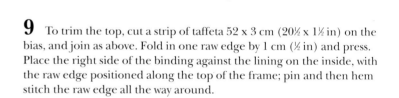

8 Fold in both raw edges by 1 cm (½ in) and press. Slip the binding over the top of the frame to rest on the neck and secure with a few dabs of glue on the underside.

9 To trim the top, cut a strip of taffeta 52 x 3 cm (20½ x 1½ in) on the bias, and join as above. Fold in one raw edge by 1 cm (½ in) and press. Place the right side of the binding against the lining on the inside, with the raw edge positioned along the top of the frame; pin and then hem stitch the raw edge all the way around.

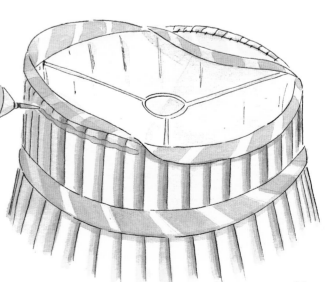

10 Now pull the folded edge over the top so that it sits around the outside and glue the flap to secure. Repeat this for the bottom using a strip measuring 83 x 3 cm (32½ x 1½ in).

equipment, materials and techniques

Basic sewing kit

To make the projects featured you will need the following: large scissors for cutting paper and card for templates, medium scissors for cutting out fabric, and small embroidery scissors for threads. Pinking shears are useful for neatening raw edges. Choose short, fine, sharp pins and strong needles. An iron is useful for pressing fabric, opening seams and marking pleats. A sewing machine will greatly speed up the making process, though it is possible to make these projects by hand if you can sew neatly . Use a safety pin for threading elastic and a blunt knitting needle for pushing out corners.

Measuring and marking tools

Accurate measuring and marking are essential aspects of lampshade making; it is vital to ensure the cover fits neatly onto the frame. Use a metal rule for straight edges and a tape measure for curves and longer lengths. For measuring and drawing small circles use a compass. For larger circles, you can make your own compass using a piece of string or tape. Insert a drawing pin through one end to mark the mid point of the circle and attach a pencil to the other end. Adjust the length of string or tape according to the diameter you require and pivot the pencil round the pin to draw the circumference. Thick paper or card is ideal for making templates. For some fitted shades and more difficult shapes, it is easier to make the template by pinning a lining material or thin calico directly onto the frame to ensure a close and accurate fit. Use an ordinary pencil, dressmaker's chalk or a removable fabric marker for marking out the pattern.

Fixing tools

Work with an appropriate adhesive; use a fabric adhesive for joining fabric to fabric and a multi-purpose glue for attaching all other types of surfaces, such as laminated fabric to a frame. Clothes pegs are handy for holding glued edges together while drying.

Laminated covers

Stiff covers are made by laminating a fabric with a self-adhesive backing. Slowly peel away the protective paper from the backing and on a flat surface carefully press the wrong side of the fabric to the sticky surface, removing any trapped air by smoothing with your hands from the middle outwards. Stiffen the fabric first and then cut out the required pattern. Self-adhesive backing is not suitable for use on an openweave fabric because dust gathers between the threads.

Fabric covers

The type of material you choose will affect the quality of light shed by the shade. Whites and light plains radiate maximum light, while dark colours and patterns obscure light. Stick to smaller repeats as large-scale patterns will be lost on all but the biggest shades. Lightweight cottons and silks are ideal for tight-fitting shades as they have give in them to aid stretching onto the frame. Geometric patterns such as checks should be cut and applied on the bias (see page 103) as it is difficult to achieve really straight vertical and horizontal lines. By positioning the checks at an angle the eye will not detect a lack of symmetry. Try to use an economical width of fabric for the shade, or piece panels together, pattern matching as necessary.

Fabric will sit better on a shaped frame if it is first cut into smaller pieces and then joined into panels. Pleated and gathered covers are deceptive; they require a lot more fabric than tight covers, often two or three times as much, so calculate amounts carefully and allow for seam allowance when you are joining pieces together.

Frames

There are all manner of shaped frames to choose from. Traditionally, frames were made of wire and then painted or covered with bias binding (see page 101) to prevent rusting, but today most are plastic-coated. When selecting a frame, make sure the style and size are appropriate to the proposed base and fittings. You can re-cover an old frame with new fabric if you strip away the old cover, but make sure there are no defects in the basic outline. Shown opposite are a selection of the most popular frames available with their technical names. You can also buy rings of different diameters, which can be combined with fabrics stiffened by lamination to make cone frames. This method allows for greater flexibility in shape and size than with ready-made wire cone frames.

Linings

These are generally used in white or cream to allow for maximum reflection of light. The lining helps to hide the struts and the outline of the bulb. Use a strong, non-tear and heat-resistant fabric such as fine Shantung or Japanese silk, satin or crepe; an alternative is acetate, although this is more liable to tear. Flame retardant spray is available for treating the lining. No lining is required on a laminated shade or when using very heavy fabrics, but with lightweight fabrics like voile or lace, lining is essential to help diffuse light and give substance to the cover.

Trimmings

Many lampshades are finished with a trimming, to hide unsightly stitching, neaten raw edges and provide decoration. Bobble fringes, braid, ribbon, rope, tassels and piping are just some options and they can be glued or hand sewn in place. Measure the section to be trimmed with a tape measure and add at least 2.5 cm (1 in) to finish the ends. For removable covers, check the washability and dyes of the trimming. It is a good idea to pre-wash all fabrics and trimmings before commencing to make up the cover, to ensure even shrinkage and to avoid colours bleeding into each other.

Frames of various shapes:

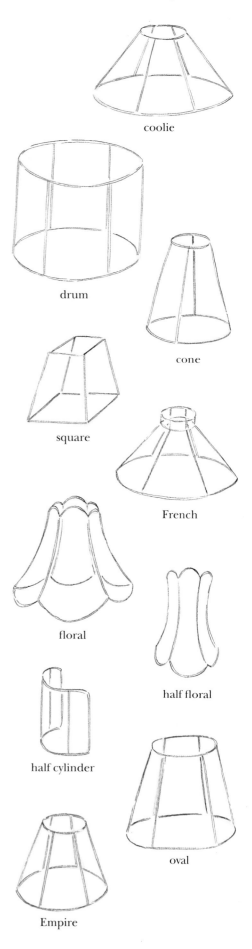

coolie

drum

cone

square

French

floral

half floral

half cylinder

oval

Empire

Fittings

When you have decided on the size and shape of your frame you must consider the internal fittings which hold the frame to the support; these are available in various sizes. Your choice of fitting will depend on the function of the shade: for instance a pendant fitting is necessary for hanging shades, whereas a reversible gimbal is used on table lamps, allowing them to be tilted when directing light on specific areas. Converters and shade carriers are available if you wish to change the height or use of your shade. Finally the size of your bulb can affect the fitting – the bulb must be hidden from view and sitting at a safe distance from the lining to avoid scorching or a fire hazard.

Bulbs

Choose a bulb according to the fitting and the size and style of the shade; the bulb should sit below the level of the top of the shade and not hang below the bottom of the shade. According to EC standards the bulb should be a least 30 mm (1¼ in) away from the inside of the shade. Be extremely careful that the bulb does not come within this recommended distance, or scorching may occur. The bulb must also be set properly in the fitting to avoid burning. For larger lamp-shades use up to 60-Watt bulb, but on smaller shades choose 40-Watt or below. Low voltage bulbs are long lasting and give off a bright light combined with low heat.

TECHNIQUES

Binding the frame

Binding not only gives a better finish if the shade is seen from above or below but provides a necessary anchor for attaching the fabric cover. In most cases, use a white or neutral binding, although sometimes a different colour may suit the design. First make sure the frame is the correct shape and free from bends as any defects will show. Use 1 cm (½ in) wide binding tape. To calculate how much tape is needed measure the length of all the sections to be covered with a tape measure and double this measurement. To bind, spiral the tape around the frame maintaining the same angle and just overlapping each previous wrap. Do not overlap by too much or the binding will become very thick. The finished binding should have a tight, smooth finish so that when you twist it between thumb and forefinger it does not slip or move.

To bind a strut, cut a length of binding tape twice the length of the strut. Turn 2.5 cm (1 in) of the tape over the top ring and with the cut end pointing down spiral the tape downwards. Finish at the base of the strut with a simple knot.

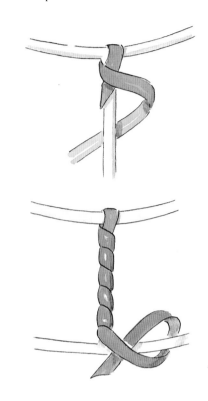

To bind the top and bottom rings of the frame, start by binding a cut end under itself next to a side strut. When you reach a join with a strut work the tape around it in a figure of eight pattern. To finish the loose end, fasten with tiny hand stitches and trim away the excess binding.

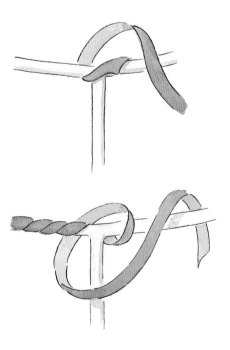

Measuring the frame

To measure any kind of cone-shaped frame, calculate the circumference around the top and bottom of the frame by measuring the relevant diameter and multiplying by three. The height of the frame is the angled (not the vertical) height between the top and bottom rings.

Making a pattern

There are two methods for making your own pattern for covering any cone-shaped frame. You can use the more exact mathematical method, involving a series of intersecting lines, as shown on pages 33 and 91. Or use this alternative method: lay a sheet of paper flat and secure the four corners by pinning to a suitable surface. Place the bare frame in one corner of the sheet, start at one strut and roll the frame across the paper in an arc until the same strut makes contact with the sheet. Rolling slowly, mark the top and bottom arcs with a pencil. Decide on a suitable all round seam allowance. Cut out the paper pattern and check its fit against the frame.

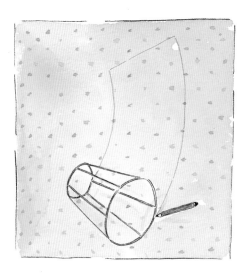

Making a drum

To make a pattern for a drum where the top and bottom rings are the same size, draw a rectangle onto a sheet of paper. The short sides correspond to the height of the shade and the long sides to the circumference; include an overlap allowance at the side.

(The circumference is three times the diameter.) Cut out the fabric and seam allowance. To glue the side of a laminated drum or cone, lie the shade seam down, place a ruler along it and overlay with a few heavy books. Leave to dry in this position.

SEWING TECHNIQUES

Running (gathering) stitch

A series of small, neat hand stitches equal in length on both sides of the fabric. Knot the ends to secure. Also used to gather cloth. For thicker fabrics and as a security against the thread breaking, sew two close parallel rows of stitches, wind the loose threads at each end around a pin and pull gently to form even gathers.

Slip stitch

Use this almost invisible stitch to join two folded edges or to attach trimmings. Knot the ends of the thread to secure. Working from right to left insert the needle and slip it through the folded fabric for about 0.5 cm (¼in), then pick up a couple of threads on the opposite fabric to join the two edges.

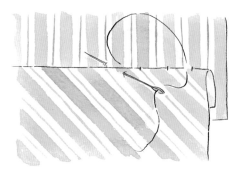

Hem stitch

Use to join fabric to binding tape on a frame or to hold a folded edge to a flat fabric, for example to finish a hem by hand. Catch a couple of threads from the flat fabric, then with the needle pointing diagonally from right to left slide it under the fabric and bring it up through the binding tape.

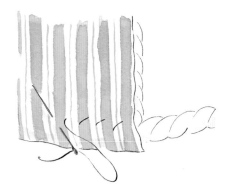

Backstitch

A continuous line of hand stitches, used as an alternative to machine stitching. Sew a line of equal straight stitches from front to back, but start each stitch by inserting the needle halfway through the previous one.

Finishing seams

On fabric not liable to fray either leave the seam allowance untrimmed or pink the raw edges with pinking shears. Otherwise finish a raw edge by oversewing or by machine with a zigzag or overlocking stitch; keep all stitches small and running over the raw edge.

French seam

This makes a very strong seam which is suitable for lightweight fabrics. Place the pieces of fabric to be joined wrong sides together with raw edges matching. Pin, baste and machine a seam 1 cm (½in) from the raw edge and trim. Turn the fabric so the right sides are now facing and press the seam line on the fold. Machine a second seam parallel to the first to enclose the raw edges. Press the seam to one side.

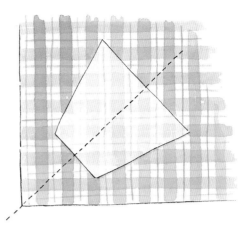

Making bias binding

Bias binding is a strip of fabric cut on the bias or diagonal grain. It is available readymade but you can create much more versatile trimmings yourself by making your own. Make sure that purchased bias binding is shrink-proof and colour-fast before sewing. To make bias strips find the bias line (see below) and use a long ruler and a pencil to mark out a series of lines parallel to the bias line, according to the width you require.

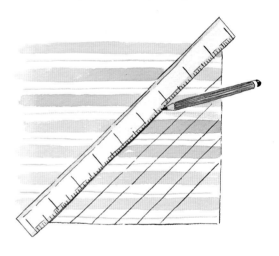

Cutting fabric on the bias

For tight covers you should cut fabric out on the bias; fabric used in this way has greater give and better stretch than fabric cut out horizontally with the direction of the grain. Before you start, make sure the fabric lends itself to this technique; some patterns may not match neatly across the angled seam produced by this method. To find the bias, take a square of fabric and fold a straight raw edge parallel to the selvedge (the non-fray woven edge), so forming a triangle. The long bottom edge of the triangle is the bias line, or true direction of bias on the fabric. Line your template up so that the bias line runs straight through the shape.

To make the long lengths that are usually required, cut out and join the bias strips along the short ends by placing them rights sides together; using a diagonal rather than a vertical seam means the strip will have greater flexibility for trimming. Note that there is a useful tool for making bias binding available from haberdashers.

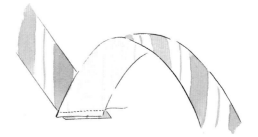

directory of suppliers

fabrics and trimmings

*Abbott & Boyd, Chelsea Harbour Design Centre, London SW10
*Alton-Brooke/Brooke London, 5 Sleaford Street, London SW8
Anta Scotland, Fearn, Tain, Ross-shire, Scotland
Laura Ashley, 27 Bagleys Lane, London SW6
Baer & Ingram, 273 Wandsworth Bridge Rd, London SW6
G. P. & J. Baker, Decorative Fabrics Gallery, 278-80 Brompton Rd, London SW3
Beaumont & Fletcher, 98 Waterford Rd, London SW6
Bennison, 16 Holbein Place, London SW1
Celia Birtwell, 71 Westbourne Park Rd, London W2
The Blue Door, 77 Church Rd, London SW13
Borderline, Chelsea Harbour Design Centre, London, SW10
*Braquenié, 251-253 Fulham Rd, London SW3
B. Brown, 79-89 Pentonville Rd, London N1
*Brunschwig & Fils, Chelsea Harbour Design Centre, London SW10
*Busby & Busby, 63 Salisbury Street, Blandford, Dorset
Nina Campbell, 9 Walton Street, London SW3
*Manuel Canovas, 2 North Terrace, Brompton Rd,

London SW3
*Chase Erwin, Chelsea Harbour Design Centre, London SW10
Chelsea Textiles, 7 Walton Street, London SW3
Jane Churchill, 151 Sloane Street, London SW3
*Claremont, 29 Elyston Street, London SW3
Colefax & Fowler, 39 Brook Street, London W1
The Conran Shop, Michelin House, 81 Fulham Rd, London SW3
*Wendy Cushing Trimmings, Chelsea Garden Market, Lots Rd, London SW10
Design Archives, Decorative Fabrics Gallery, 278–80 Brompton Rd, London SW3
Designers Guild, 277 Kings Rd, London SW3
Thomas Dare, 431 Kings Rd, London SW3
*Donghia, Chelsea Harbour Design Centre, London SW10
*Jason D'Souza, Chelsea Harbour Design Centre, London SW10
*Guy Evans, 96 Great Titchfield Street, London W1
Fardis, Decorative Fabrics Gallery, 278-80 Brompton Rd, London SW3
Firifiss, Decorative Fabrics Gallery, 278–80 Brompton Rd, London SW3
Anna French, 343 Kings Rd, London SW3
*Pierre Frey, 251-253 Fulham Rd, London SW3
*Mary Fox Linton, Chelsea Harbour Design Centre,

London SW10
Hill & Knowles, Chelsea Harbour Design Centre, London SW10
Hodsoll McKenzie, 52 Pimlico Rd, London SW1
*JAB International, Chelsea Harbour Design Centre, London SW10
Cath Kidston, 8 Clarendon Cross, London W11
Knickerbean, PO Box 36, Thetford, Norfolk
Ralph Lauren Home Collection, Harvey Nichols, London SW1
*Lee Jofa, Chelsea Harbour Design Centre, London SW10
*Lelievre, 101 Cleveland Street, London W1
John Lewis, Oxford Street, London W1
Lewis & Wood, 48a Pimlico Rd, London SW1
Liberty, 210 Regent Street, London W1
*Malabar Cotton Co, The Coach House Bakery Place, 119 Altenburg Gardens, London SW11
Ian Mankin, 109 Regents Park Rd, London NW1
*Marvic, 12-14 Mortimer Street, London W1
Monkwell, Decorative Fabrics Gallery, 278-80 Brompton Rd, London SW3
Mulberry Home, 76 Chelsea Manor Street, London SW3
*Henry Newbery Trimmings, 18 Newman St, London W1
*Nobilis Fontan, 1 and 2 Cedar Studios, 45 Glebe Place, London SW3

Osborne & Little, 304-308 Kings Rd, London SW3
*Paper Moon, 53 Fairfax Rd, London NW6
Parkertex, Decorative Fabrics Gallery, 278-80 Brompton Rd, London SW3
*Percheron, 97-99 Cleveland Street, London W1
*Pongees, 28-30 Hoxton Square, London N1
*Ramm, Son & Crocker, Chelsea Harbour Design Centre, London SW10
Romo, Lowmoor Rd, Kirkby-in-Ashfield, Notts
V.V. Rouleaux, 10 Symons Street, London SW3
*Sahco Hesslein, Chelsea Harbour Design Centre, London SW10
Sanderson, 112-120 Brompton Rd, London SW3
*Ian Sanderson, Chelsea Harbour Design Centre, London SW10
Shaker 322 King's Rd, London SW3
George Spencer, 4 East Halkin Street, London SW1
John Stefanidis, 261 Fulham Rd, London SW3
Timney Fowler, 388 Kings Rd, London SW3
*Tissunique, Chelsea Harbour Design Centre, London SW10
*Titley & Marr, Chelsea Harbour Design Centre, London SW10
Today Interiors, 122 Fulham Rd, London SW3

*Turnell & Gigon, Chelsea Harbour Design Centre, London SW10
*Warner Fabrics, Chelsea Harbour Design Centre, London SW10
*Watts of Westminster, Chelsea Harbour Design Centre, London SW10
*Brian Yates, Chelsea Harbour Design Centre, London SW10
*Zimmer & Rohde, Chelsea Harbour Design Centre, London SW10
Zoffany, 63 South Audley Street, London W1

lamps

Acres Farm, Bradfield, Berkshire
Besselink & Jones, 99 Walton Street, London SW3
Bella Figura, Decoy Farm, Old Church Rd, Melton, Suffolk
The Blue Door as above
Designers Guild as above
The Dining Room Shop, 64 White Hart Lane, London SW13
Elizabeth Eaton, 85 Bourne Street, London SW1
Extraordinary Design, 77 Conway Rd, London N14
Hannah Gordon Designs, 16 Harbord Street, London SW6
Habitat, 196 Tottenham Court Rd, London W1
Heal's, 196 Tottenham Court Rd, London W1
John Lewis as above

Liberty as above
Mr Light, 279 Kings Rd, London W1
Lion Witch & Lampshade, 89 Ebury Street, London SW1
Nimbus Design, High Hall, Wimborne, Dorset
Patrick Quiggly, 52 Rupert Street, London W1
Purves & Purves, 80–81 & 83 Tottenham Court Rd, London W1
Renwick & Clarke, 190 Ebury Street, London SW1
Sanderson as above
*Tindle, 168 Wandsworth Bridge Rd, London SW6
*Vaughan, 156 Wandsworth Bridge Rd, London SW6
Robert Wyatt, 13 The Shrubbery, Grosvenor Rd, Wanstead, London E11

bespoke lampshades

Besselink & Jones as above
Bella Figura as above
Sally Harclerode at H & H Associates, 18 Connaught Drive, NW11
Lion Witch & Lampshade as above
*M&F Products, Wandle Mills, Wandle Rd, Beddington, Croydon (framemakers)
Renwick & Clarke as above
Tindle as above
Vaughan as above
Robert Wyatt as above

* denotes trade only; contact for your nearest supplier

credits

front cover: from top to bottom: fabric Ian Mankin; fabric Pierre Frey, trimming Colefax & Fowler; fabric Pierre Frey; plain red silk Brunschwig & Fils, striped silk Manuel Canovas; fabric Pierre Frey; all shades made by Vaughan

page 1   checked and plain thin silk taffeta shade by Anna Thomas

page 2   from top to bottom: shade made by Sally Harclerode, fabric from Designers Guild, piping from V.V. Rouleaux; shade made by Bella Figura, fabric from Baer & Ingram, trimming from Jane Churchill ; shade made by Sally Harclerode, fabric from Osborne & Little; shade made by Robert Wyatt, fabric from Ian Mankin

page 4   from left to right: shade made by Robert Wyatt, ribbon by V.V. Rouleaux; shades made by Acres Farm, fabric from Ian Mankin, shade made by Robert Wyatt

page 5   from left to right: shade by Vaughan, fabric from Manuel Canovas; shade by Vaughan, fabric from Manuel Canovas; shade made by Robert Wyatt, fabric from Sanderson, leather from John Lewis

page 6   shade made by Robert Wyatt, fabric from JAB, trimming from V. V. Rouleaux

page 7   clockwise from bottom left: shade made by Tindle, fabric from Jane Churchill; shade made by Robert Wyatt, fabric from Design Archives; shade made by Robert Wyatt, fabric from Sanderson, shade made by Vaughan, fabric from Jane Churchill ; shade made by Robert Wyatt, fabric from Designers Guild; shade made by Vaughan, fabric from Sanderson

projects: *laminated checked square:* made by Robert Wyatt. base from Hannah Gordon Designs, fabric from The Blue Door • *pleated coolie:* made by Sally Harclerode, silk from Pongees *tall madras bowed oval:* made by Robert Wyatt, fabric from JAB, trimming by V. V. Rouleaux

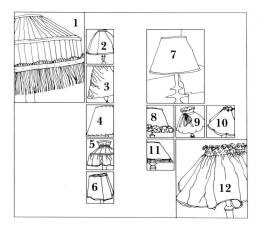

projects: *skirted pictorial print:* made by Bella Figura, fabric from Baer & Ingram, trimming from Jane Churchill • *hessian half shade:* made by Robert Wyatt • *raw and ruffled:* shade from Renwick & Clarke • *woven ribbons:* made by Robert Wyatt, ribbon from V. V. Rouleaux • *tutu in voile:* shade from Vaughan

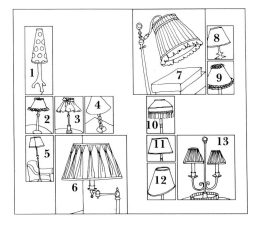

projects: *box-pleated conical shade:* fabric from Manuel Canovas, base and shade by Vaughan • *smocked patterned shade:* shade from The Dining Room Shop • *covered shade:* shade from Vaughan • *scalloped crown:* made by Robert Wyatt, fabric from The Blue Door

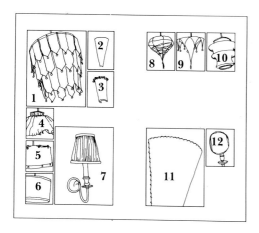

wall and ceiling lamps pages 62–63
1 shade supplied by Nimbus Designs
2, 11 shade from Patrick Quiggly
3 shade made by Robert Wyatt, fabric from Chelsea Textiles, fringe from Osborne & Little
4 shade made by Vaughan, fabric from Celia Birtwell
5 shade by Robert Wyatt
6 shade by Robert Wyatt, hessian from B. Brown
7 shade and wall bracket from Vaughan, fabric from Sanderson
8 shade from Mr Light
9, 10 shade from Extraordinary Design
12 shade made by Tindle, fabric from Chelsea Textiles.

projects: *linen loose cover:* made by Hänsi Schneider, fabric from Sahco Hesslein • *gingham in gathers:* shade by Vaughan, fabric from Ian Mankin, trimming from V. V. Rouleaux • *chandelier candle shades:* shades made by Acres Farm, fabric from Ian Mankin • *two-tiered hanging lamp:* The Blue Door • *striped wall shield:* shade by Sally Harclerode, fabric from Manuel Canovas

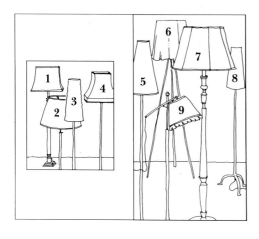

floor lamps pages 84–85
1 shade made by Robert Wyatt, fabric by Schumacher for Turnell & Gigon, trimming from Liberty, base from Vaughan.
2 shade made by Bella Figura, fabric from Monkwell., base from Bella Figura
3 shade and base from Mr Light
4 shade from Tindle, base from Mr Light
5 shade made by Robert Wyatt, fabric from JAB, base from Mr Light
6 shade and base from Purves & Purves
7 shade made by Bella Figura, fabric from Parkertex, base from Vaughan
8 shade and base from Mr Light
9 shade made by Vaughan, fabric from Knickerbean, base from Bella Figura

projects: *stripes round a drum:* made by Robert Wyatt, fabric from Monkwell, trimming from Jane Churchill, base from Habitat • *leather stitched chimney:* made by Robert Wyatt, fabric from Sanderson, leather from John Lewis • *pleated cone with collar:* made by Vaughan, fabric from Manuel Canovas

page 98 shade from Besselink & Jones
page 99 all shades made by Robert Wyatt, green fabric from John Stefanidis, red fabric from The Blue Door, purple fabric from Manuel Canovas
page 104 shade from The Blue Door
page 105 shade made by Sally Harclerode, fabric from Designers Guild, base from Besselink & Jones
page 109 shade made by Sally Harclerode, fabric from Designers Guild, piping from V. V. Rouleaux, base from The Blue Door
page 110 shade from Renwick & Clarke
page 111 shade from Renwick & Clarke
page 112 shade and base by Robert Wyatt, fabric from Ian Mankin, bobble fringe from Jane Churchill
endpapers: shade made by Vaughan, fabric from Colefax & Fowler

glossary

Basting
Large straight stitches used to fasten layers of fabric in position temporarily.

Basting thread
Also tacking thread. Usually made of cotton and worked in a loose stitch. Use a contrasting colour to show up against your material.

Bias binding tape or strip
Also crossway strip: a strip cut obliquely from selvedge to selvedge for added strength. Used to bind frames, edges or to enclose piping cord.

Bobble fringe
Tufted ball attached to a length of trimming.

Box pleat
A symmetrical pleat with fabric turned in at each side.

Braid
A woven ribbon used to trim or edge pillows and cushions.

Casing
An enclosing cover used for both decorative and protective purposes.

Gathers
Puckers or folds made in cloth by drawing on a loosely stitched thread.

Gimbal fitting
The device attached to the inside of a frame; used to fit the shade to the base and the bulb.

Gimp
A twist of fabric, sometimes stiffened with cord or wire.

Gingham
A fine cotton cloth of Indian origin usually woven in stripes or checks.

Grain
The pattern of lines on a fabric, according to the weave.

Hem
A border or cut edge of cloth, usually turned under and sewn in place.

Hessian
Also burlap. A strong, coarse fabric made of jute or hemp fibres. Most commonly used for sacking and in upholstery.

Hole punch
Special tool used to pierce holes in a material.

Interfacing
Special material used to line and stiffen a fabric; either sewn or ironed in place.

Knife pleat
A narrow sharply folded pleat with a straight edge.

Laminate
A thin protective covering, bonded to a material.

Leather thong
A narrow strip of leather used as a lace.

Madras cotton
Striped and checked fine Indian cotton, commonly identified by its bright colours.

Notch
A small V-shaped cut into the edge of a fabric.

Organza
A thin, transparent, plain-woven silk or synthetic fabric with a stiff finish.

Pinking shears
Scissors with notched blades used for cutting a zigzag edge for decoration or finishing.

Pleat
A double fold or crease, pressed or stitched in place.

Provençal print
French country print on cotton, characterized by small brightly coloured motifs.

Raw edge
The cut edge of fabric, without selvedge or hem; often needs finishing to prevent fraying.

Ruffle
A gathered strip of cloth used as a trimming.

Score
To mark a line by scratching the surface.

Seam allowance
The narrow strip of raw-edged fabric left when making a seam, to allow for fraying.

Seam line
The line formed when two pieces of material are stitched together.

Selvedge
The defined warp edge of the fabric, specially woven to prevent unravelling.

Snip
A small cut made in a piece of material with scissors.

Strut
A bar fitted into a frame to strengthen against pressure.

Template
A shape made of card or paper, used to mark specific outlines on fabric.

Toile
Plain cloth on its own or in *toile de Jouy* to mean fabric embellished with pictorial scenes.

Undershade
A shade usually made of stiff card and used as a base for a more decorative outer covering.

Width
The distance from selvedge to selvedge on any fabric. The standard widths for fabric are 90 cm (36 in), 115 cm (45 in) and 150 cm (60 in).

index

acknowledgements

Many, many thanks to all the suppliers who so kindly helped us with this book: all the fabric companies who gave us their gorgeous fabrics and trimmings, all those who lent us lamp bases and shades. To Lucy Vaughan and all who work at Vaughan, I thank for all their patience and help while I drove them crazy borrowing their lovely lamps and shades. To Robert Wyatt for all his great ideas and lampshades and help on the technical side – many thanks. Sally Harclerode made some exquisite shades for us – thank you. And to Betty Hanley, the doyenne of beautiful lampshades, who is now retired but by whose training many people are still producing bespoke lampshades.

Thanks to Annie Stevens and Anna Thomas for letting us invade their houses to take many of the photographs; to Catherine Coombes who tirelessly helped with this book and kept everyone at home happy at the same time; to James Merrell for his wonderful photographs; to a really great and professional team at Ryland Peters & Small – well done; to David and Harry always and forever.

dedication

In memory of my father and Carolyn Brunton

soft furnishing workbooks

lampshades